Grading Hardwood (Understanding AS2082)

EDGAR (TED) STUBBERSFIELD

Copyright: Rachel Stubbersfield, 2013
All rights reserved
IBN: 0992425921
IBN 13: 978-0-9924259-2-0

Contents

Acknowledgements i
Introduction 1
Chapter 1. Structural Grades of Hardwood 2
    Structural Grade 1 6
    Structural Grade 2 (simplified rules) 7
    Structural Grade 3 (simplified rules) 8
    Structural Grade 4 (simplified rules) 9
    Illustrations of Defects 10
        Sawing Tolerance 10
        Knots 11
        Borer holes 14
        Termite Galleries 14
        Slope of Grain 15
        Heart 16
        Gum veins 18
        Gum, Latex, Resin Pockets 19
        End Splits 20
        Checks 21
        Shakes 21
        Rot 23
        Want and Wane 24
        Lyctus Susceptible Sapwood 25
        Straightness 26
    Appearance Grades 27
    Durability, the Great Omission 28
Chapter 2. Section 1 of AS2082 31
    1.1.2 Scope and Application of AS2082 31
    1.3 Referenced Documents 32
        AS2878 Timber - Classification into strength groups 32
        AS1604.1 Specification for preservative treatment 33
        AS1148 Nomenclature - Australian, New Zealand and imported species 33
        A/NZS 4491 Timber-Glossary of terms in timber related Standards 37
    1.4 Definitions 37
        1.4.3 Exceptionally low density material 38

  1.4.4 Heart 38

 1.5 Timber Species and Stress Grades 39

 1.6 Structural Grades of Hardwood 40

 1.7 Sizes and Tolerances 40

  Rough Sawn Green Off Saw 40

  Sized Green Off Saw 41

  Dressed Green Off Saw 41

  Dressed Seasoned 41

  Note on Unit Shrinkage 42

  1.7.3 Special Straightness requirements 43

 1.8 Moisture Content 43

Chapter 3. Section 3 A17 46

Matters Arising 47

 F17 and F11 KD Hardwood Specification 47

 F17 Seasoned Decking 49

 Specifying Timber Handrail 49

Chapter 4. Alternate Standards 51

 AS3818.6 Visually graded Decking for wharves and bridges 51

 AS3818.7 Visually Graded Large Section Timbers 51

 AS2796.1 Timber – Hardwood – Sawn and milled products 52

 Specifications for Recycled Timber 53

Chapter 5. How effective is grading to AS2082? 58

Chapter 6. Case Histories 60

 Sunshine Plaza Deck 60

 Bremmer River Boardwalk, Ipswich 66

Conclusion 70

Appendix 1. A Personal Experience with Grading 71

Appendix 2. A Personal Experience with Straightness 71

Source of Images 72

Abbreviations 72

References 73

About the Author 76

Acknowledgements

When writing this book I have drawn upon a lifetime in the hardwood sawmilling industry. I appreciate the assistance provided by people in my industry. Some have drawn from their experience and offered guidance on how this book could be improved others provided valuable, hard to obtain documents.

Geoff Stringer B.Eng. (Hons),
Technical Manager, Hyne and Son Pty Limited

Bill Thorne
Wholesale Manager Parkside Timbers

Errol Wildman, B. Bus
Formerly proprietor of Homestead Timbers, Wandoan Queensland.

While this book does not claim to represent the views of the Department of Agriculture, Fisheries and Forestry. The assistance of two of its officers is especially acknowledged.

Gary Hopewell AD AppSc (Forestry), MSc (WoodSc)
Senior Scientist, Forest Product Innovations
Agri-Science Queensland

Bill Atyeo BSc(Hons), Grad Dip Ed
Research Scientist
Agri-Science Queensland.

Introduction

As a young man, I witnessed the transition of timber from being a traditional product used by conscientious craftsmen to becoming an "engineered" product used by unskilled and often uncaring contractors. The industry is vastly different now to the one I was introduced to. Back then, the person who purchased the timber was the one who used it and, if the timber was not to their standard, they brought it back, demanding, with expletives, that you replace it. These builders took pride in what they produced. The normal situation now is that a purchaser in an office, far from the project, after tracking down the lowest price for the grade specified orders the timber. A team of contract builders turns up on site and uses that timber as quickly as possible as they have been forced to accept a low price for their services. Delays through rejecting timber just cannot be accepted so what is supplied is what is used. The job just has to be "good enough"; the completed home was no longer a reflection of them (or perhaps, more than ever it is a reflection).

"Good enough", the term driving most timber applications, could also be rephrased as the more professionally sounding "serviceability". Serviceability, the ability of the timber to provide good/adequate service, is mentioned twice in AS2082-2010 but this can be a misleading statement. Provide good service as what? A 100x100 mm at 2.4 m long purchased at a low price from a fencing supplier, might give adequate service as a fence post many metres from the house. That same piece will probably be very unsuitable as a verandah post, the first item noticed when visiting the house and reflecting the quality of everything that is hidden behind a roof and dry wall sheeting.

When timber was "engineered" it moved forward without taking with it almost 200 years of acquired knowledge of what was best practice in the specification, supply and use of hardwood. One timber industry magazine said at the time (late seventies) that millers did not need to fear the introductions of F ratings as now they could sell product that was previously considered unsaleable. This small book is, in part, an attempt to recapture what has been lost and hopefully inspire professional designers to incorporate the traditional wisdom encapsulated in the dying art of timber use as an equal alongside the science.

The outline of this book is first to look at Section 2 of AS2082 where the four structural grades are defined and illustrate the main defects that are encountered, then emphasise the great omission to the standard, that of durability. The book will then look at Section 1 and 3 of the Standard and discuss matters that are not straightforward. Related matters that are not addressed under AS2082 are then reviewed. The book will conclude with grading requirements for specialised products and then include some case studies.

This book is not a substitute for purchasing the AS2082 but is intended to be read alongside the standard.

The information shown herein does not constitute a complete design so a Consulting Engineer with skills in both timber design and foundation systems should be engaged for the structural and foundation design

Chapter 1. Structural Grades of Hardwood

There are over 200 species of hardwood milled commercially in Australia. Properties of sawn timber that look very similar can be extremely diverse in all their properties, not just the structural ones. In the 1940's the first attempts were made to group species of similar properties for design purposes. Four hypothetical species were invented called A, B, C & D. Unfortunately, these categories proved inadequate as:
- All the properties for all grades had not been determined and
- They did not suit plantation pine.

The A to D category was superseded in 1965 as
- There was a need for a more inclusive system
- Much more data on species properties had been gathered and
- A system was needed that accurately reflected the structural properties of the different species.

The later research had come to appreciate how different types of natural feature and their size, i.e. the grade, affected stiffness. While it was known that strength varied with the grade it was originally assumed that the MOE remained constant across a species irrespective of grade. The new testing demonstrated that stiffness also varied with grade which then meant that working stresses[1] had to be modified. The opportunity had arisen to develop a more flexible and rational system that also correlated with mechanically graded timber.

Such a system was sorely needed. The colloquial term "dogs breakfast" comes to mind when trying to describe the grading that was recognised under the Australian Standards at the time of this review. It was possible to order timber as:
- Building grade
- Standard grade
- Select graded of
- Merchantable grade
- Select merchantable grade
- Engineering grade
- Standard engineering grade
- Select engineering grade
- Structural grade 1
- Structural grade 2
- Light scantling grade and
- Standard building grade

This plethora of terms said very little about structural adequacy of the timber. They frequently "convey[ed] incorrect impressions of the suitability of timber ordered or specified for specific structural purposes".[2] On top of this the same terms, "select" and "standard" was being used for appearance grade timbers as well as framing timbers which was causing confusion.

---

[1] During the 1990's Australia changed from working stress to limit state engineering.
[2] Kloot, H. The Strength Group and Stress Grade Systems in CSIRO Forest Products Newsletter No 394 (CSIRO: South Melbourne, 1973) 2.

The A to D grouping was replaced with seven Strength Groups (S1 to S7) for unseasoned timber which gave the flexibility to now include not only the hardwoods but also the exotic plantation species. These could now be covered with 12 sets of working stresses instead of the previous 28. Along with the introduction of new Strength Groups, a new term was introduced, Stress Grades. This was defined as "a grading index of the ability of a piece of timber to perform satisfactorily in a structural capacity in a building."[3] These Stress Grades were designated as a number with an F in front e.g. F14 which "indicated that for such a grade of material the basic working stress in bending is approximately 14 megapascals (MPa). Table One shows the values for each grade at the time they were introduced.

Stress Grade	Type of Stress				Modulus of Elasticity
	Bending	Tension parallel to grain	Shear in Bending	Compression parallel to grain	
F34	34.5	25.5	2.45	26.0	21500
F27	27.5	22.0	2.05	20.5	18500
F22	22.0	17.0	1.7	16.5	16000
F17	17.0	14,0	1.45	13.0	14000
F14	14.0	11.0	1.25	10.5	12500
F11	11.0	8.6	1.05	8.3	10500
F8	8.6	6.9	0.86	6.6	9100
F7	6.9	5.5	0.72	5.2	7900
F5	5.5	4.3	0.62	4.1	6900
F4	4.3	3.4	0.52	3.3	6100
F3	3.4	2.8	0.43	2.6	5200
F2	2.8	2.2	0.36	2.1	4500

Table 1. Basic Working Stresses and Modulus of Elasticity (MPa).[4]

Despite the move away from working stress to limit state engineering the F designations were retained as they were convenient.

With the adoption of new F designation it was intended that:
- terms that were purely descriptive could be done away with
- There would be a interlocking system of Strength Groups, visual grades and stress grades.

The market at that time had been overwhelmingly based on unseasoned products but interest was being generated in gluelam beams and seasoned framing was seen as a future development. (Only radiata was required to be seasoned at that stage). It was decided to also establish a sound basis for the design of seasoned timbers. The values for unseasoned timber were ignored and each species were re-tested in their kiln dried (12% moisture) state. Eight categories were established with the prefix SD. This meant that each species now had two Strength Groups. It was thought that this "should not present any significant practical difficulties".[5] This has not proved the case.[6] The two Strength Groups do have the

---
[3] Kloot, *Strength...*, 2.
[4] Kloot, *Strength...*, 3.
[5] Kloot, *Strength...*, 3.

advantage of identifying those species that have considerable increase in their properties when dried. This allows these species to be used more efficiently.

The F ratings are based on matching the Strength Group of a species[7] with one of the four Structural Grades in AS2082. These are applied in exactly the same way for unseasoned an seasoned hardwood. The Structural Grades are meant to represent a percentage of the strength of timber when free of any natural feature. Those percentages are found in Table Two. Note how low the percentage is for some grades. What makes the difference in percentage is the amount of natural feature, such as knots, that each of the grades allow.

When produced from the timbers of South East Queensland, these lower F grades are visually unacceptable.[9] Yet we see some professional designers, who just see a number with an F in front of it, asking for grades that are far lower than 38% of the strength of solid timber[10]. Visually and structurally they are appalling.

Structural Grade:	% of clear wood strength
No. 1	75%
No. 2	60%
No. 3	48%
No. 4	38%

Table 2. Structural grades as a percentage of solid wood.[8]

There are, however, Structural Appearance Grades[11] but they only partly address the issue of appearance and are suited for internal use only and with non-discerning clients[12]. The suitability of AS2082 to specify handrails is examined[13] and found deficient.

Conformance to AS2082 does not ensure fitness for purpose nor does non-conformance necessarily preclude it from use. Years ago I was serving on a standards committee and one member would continually bring up the need for great care in the wording as this would be read by an Indian[14] engineer with little understanding of what he is reading and with no disposition to be flexible. He gave the case of a long 200x150 mm member that he had been called in to grade. It had previously been rejected by one of his so called "Indian engineers" for having a couple of millimeters too much bow. This member was intended as a kerb on a wharf and was a very difficult size to cut and replace. Despite repeated calls he did not arrive to re-grade the piece until the weather changed to a cool spell. He then re-measured the bow, and, with the change in the weather, it had come back into grade much to the astonishment of the person who rejected it. He is still under the impression he measured incorrectly. A very frustrated builder then took the kerb, placed it with the bow up drilled through the centre, put a bolt through and tightened it, straightening it as he went.

---

[6] Refer to the chapter "Matters Arising: where this is discussed.
[7] This is expanded upon in comments on Clause 1.3 of AS2082-2007.
[8] Wood Solutions. *Visual Stress Grading*. URL: https://www.woodsolutions.com.au/articles/visual-stress-grading Date Accessed: 19 October 2020.
[9] Refer to Appendix 1 for an example of F grades not meeting visual expectation.
[10] Refer to my comments on F14 and F17 KD specification.
[11] AS2082-2007 Clause 2.5.
[12] I am thinking of heartache I encountered with a job where the clients were solicitors and the wife had an extreme emotional response to a small amount of tight gum vein when the standard allows unlimited amounts in F27 KD blackbutt.
[13] Refer to Matters Arrising – Specifying Handrail.
[14] I apologise to my Indian readers. While the bureaucratic inflexibility of officials in the subcontinent is the making of legends it is by no means an Indian only quality. We have all seen it far too often in Australian born and bred professionals.

What follows are simplified grading rules for the four Structural Grades. When reading these rules it is important "engage your brain" with all its faculties for reason about the end use of the piece that is being graded. In the discussion of the natural features which follows I try to give some guidance for going beyond the wording of AS2082 and grading for fitness for purpose.

Structural Grade 1 (simplified rules)[15]

Producing from the following species		
	Unseasoned	Seasoned
Tallowwood	F27	F34
Spotted gum	F22	F34
Sydney blue gum	F17	F27
Jarrah	F14	F22

Fault	Permitted extent
Fractures and splits	Only end splits are allowed
Sawing Tolerance	+ or – 3 mm
Knots	One seventh of face
Borer holes	12 per 100x100 mm (up to 3 mm)
Termite galleries	Enclosed - not permitted, open - as for want and wane .
Slope of grain	1 in 15 (jarrah 1 in 12)
Heart[16]	Not permitted where smaller dimension under 175 mm. Limited to inner one third for other sizes. Permitted in limited species[17] to be one twentieth of cross section.
Tight gum veins	Max one and a half times the length in aggregate. One quarter the length if extending face to face
Loose gum veins and included bark	One tenth the length and 3 mm max measured radially. Not extending from face to face
Gum pockets	Up to three times the width to a max. 300 mm. On one face, a quarter of the width up to 12 mm
End splits	The width but exceeding 100 mm in aggregate (per end)
Checks	Up to 3 mm wide and one quarter the length
Rot	3 mm deep and 150x100 mm per 2.0m length
Want and wane, Lyctus susceptible sapwood	One tenth of the cross section

---

[15] From AS2082 -2007 2.1
[16] Refer to notes Included Heart where the implications of the change of definition of heart in AS2082 are discussed in detail.
[17] These are blackbutt, grey box, forest red gum, spotted gum, grey ironbark, broad and narrow leaved red ironbark.

Structural Grade 2 (simplified rules)[18]

Producing from the following species		
	Unseasoned	Seasoned
Tallowwood	F22	F27
Spotted gum	F17	F27
Sydney blue gum	F14	F22
Jarrah	F11	F17

Fault	Permitted extent
Fractures and splits	Only end splits are allowed
Sawing tolerance	+ or – 3 mm
Knots	One quarter of face
Borer holes	20 per 100x100 mm (up to 3 mm)
Termite galleries	Enclosed - not permitted, open - as for want and wane.
Slope of grain	1 in 10 (jarrah 1 in 8)
Heart[19]	Not permitted where smaller dimension under 175 mm. Limited to inner one third for other sizes. Permitted in limited species[20] to be one ninth of cross section.
Tight gum veins	Unlimited
Loose gum veins and included bark	One sixth of the length and 3 mm max. measured radially. Not extending from face to face
Gum pockets	Length: Up to three times the width plus 300 mm. Width on one face: one third of the width up to 12 mm
End splits	Width but not exceeding 100 mm in aggregate (per end)
Checks	Up to 3 mm wide and one third of the length
Rot	3 mm deep and 150x100 mm per 2.0 m length
Want and wane, Lyctus susceptible sapwood	One fifth of the cross section

---

[18] From AS2082 -2007 2.2
[19] Refer to notes Included Heart where the implications of the change of definition of heart in AS2082 are discussed in detail.
[20] These are blackbutt, grey box, forest red gum, spotted gum, grey ironbark, broad and narrow leaved red ironbark.

Structural Grade 3 (simplified rules)[21]

Producing from the following species		
	Unseasoned	Seasoned
Tallowwood	F17	F22
Spotted gum	F14	F22
Sydney blue gum	F11	F17
Jarrah	F8	F14

Fault	Permitted Extent
Fractures and splits	Only end splits are allowed
Sawing tolerance	+ or – 3 mm
Knots	One third of the face
Borer holes	Unlimited per 100x100 mm (up to 3 mm)
Termite galleries	Enclosed: Not permitted, Open: As for want and wane
Slope of grain	1 in 8 (jarrah 1 in 6)
Heart[22]	Not permitted where smaller dimension under 175 mm. Limited to inner one third for other sizes. Permitted in limited species[23] to be one sixth of cross section.
Tight gum veins	Unlimited.
Loose gum veins and included bark	One quarter the length and 3 mm max measured radially. Not extending from face to face
Gum pockets	Length: up to three times the width to a max. 300 mm. Width on one face: one half of the width up to 25 mm
End splits	One and half times width but not exceeding 150 mm in aggregate (per end)
Checks	Up to 3 mm wide and one half the length
Rot	3 mm deep and 150x100 mm per 2.0m length
Want and wane, Lyctus susceptible sapwood	One fifth of the cross section

---

[21] From AS2082 -2007 2.3
[22] Refer to notes Included Heart where the implications of the change of definition of heart in AS2082 are discussed in detail.
[23] These are blackbutt, grey box, forest red gum, spotted gum, grey ironbark, broad and narrow leaved red ironbark.

Structural Grade 4 (simplified rules)[24]

Producing from the following species		
	Unseasoned	Seasoned
Tallowwood	F11	F17
Spotted gum	F11	F17
Sydney blue gum	F8	F14
Jarrah	F7	F11

Fault	Permitted Extent
Fractures and splits	Only end splits are allowed
Sawing tolerance	+ or – 3 mm
Knots	Three eighths of face
Borer holes	unlimited (up to 3 mm)
Termite galleries	Enclosed: Not permitted, Open: As for want and wane
Slope of grain	1 in 6, jarrah included
Heart[25]	Not permitted where smaller dimension under 175 mm. Limited to inner one third for other sizes. Permitted in limited species[26] to be one third of cross section.
Tight gum veins	unlimited
Loose gum veins and included bark	One third the length and 3 mm max. measured radially. Not extending from face to face
Gum pockets	Up to three times the width to a Max. 300 mm. On one face, a half of the width up to 30 mm
End splits	One and half times width but not exceeding 150 mm in aggregate (per end)
Checks	Up to 3 mm wide and one half the length
Rot	3 mm deep and 150x100 mm per 2.0m length
Want and wane, Lyctus susceptible sapwood	One fifth of the cross section

---

[24] From AS2082 -2007 2.4
[25] Refer to notes Included Heart where the implications of the change of definition of heart in AS2082 are discussed in detail.
[26] These are blackbutt, grey box, forest red gum, spotted gum, grey ironbark, broad and narrow leaved red ironbark.

Illustrations of Defects

Sawing Tolerance

| Figure 1. 161 mm, 11 mm over nominal size. | Figure 2. 143 mm, 7 mm under nominal size. |

An allowance in the width and thickness of plus or minus 3 mm for all grades, sizes and lengths is to be made with green off saw timber. This is optimistic on larger sizes. The 1979 standard was more realistic which allowed 9 mm oversize for sizes 200 mm and larger for lengths up to 6.0 m and 12 mm for lengths longer than 6.0 m.[27] 12 mm is excessive but somewhere in-between is sustainable.

The two boards shown, both nominally 150 mm wide, appear out of grade but are acceptable for their intended purpose. The piece in Figure 1 is intended as a kiln dried product and as it has a higher shrinkage than normal was cut 9 mm oversize to compensate. The board was 161 mm wide so in actual fact it was only 2 mm oversize. Cutting intentionally oversize boards within the 3 mm oversize tolerance is still important as the dressing process requires uniform accurately sized boards for it to flow smoothly.[28] Though the board in figure 2 is undersize by 7 mm this is largely due to shrinkage and as the product is also going to be kiln dried this would be considered as part of the drying process.

Sizes in hardwood are very complex and this section is expanded upon in my discussion of clause 1.7 of AS2082-2007

---

[27] AS2082-1979 Clause 1.6.2. I have processed a considerable amount of 200x200 mm from different mills and if we rejected every piece that was more than 3 mm oversize we would have had no suppliers. In my book, *The Seven Deadly Sins of Timber Design* I explain how to deal with this sawing tolerance in a 200x200 mm.

[28] To finish a standard 136 mm, one of the side heads of the planer has remove 9-10 mm off this board after drying. With 3 mm oversize this is at least 12 mm to be removed. The planer is working very hard indeed.

Knots

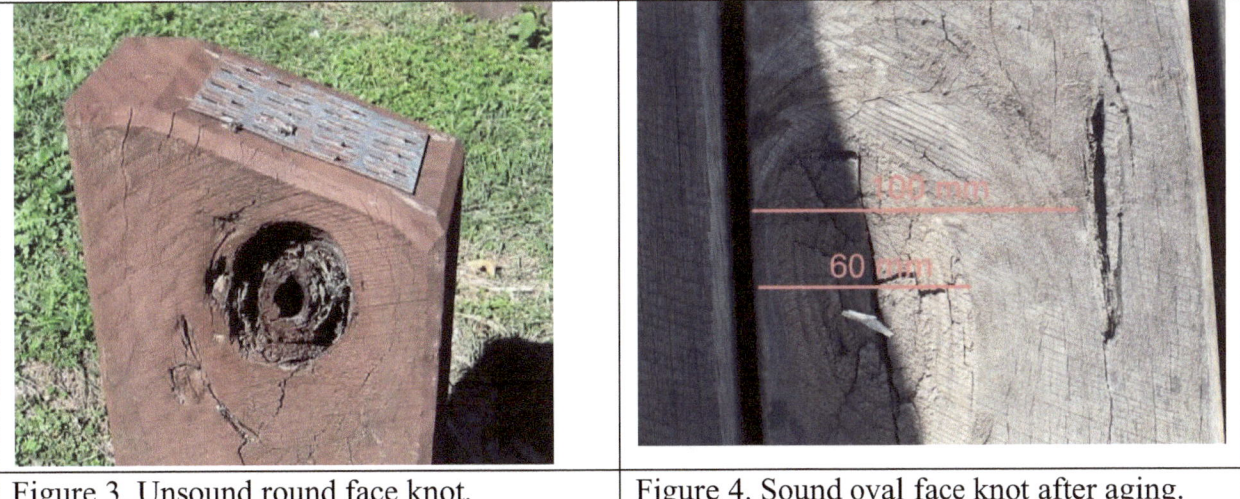

| Figure 3. Unsound round face knot. | Figure 4. Sound oval face knot after aging. |

Two types of knot are recognised, sound and unsound which are found in round, oval, encasement and arris format. These can occur in conjunction with other permissible defects such as being within the sawing tolerance and having want and wane. Figures 3 and 4 show that sound and unsound knots are very different in appearance yet despite that they are treated the same. When new, the knot in Figure 4 would have appeared completely sound but after being exposed to the weather it has starburst allowing moisture to enter. Time is all that differentiates the effect of the knot in Figure 3 from Figure 4.

Figure 4 illustrates the difficulty sometimes found in measuring the width of a knot. The primary knot in this piece of 145 mm wide decking in spotted gum decking is only 60 mm across (all measurements are made perpendicular to the edge). Even so this is 40% of the width of the timber. The lowest grade, Structural 4 producing F11 would have permitted a knot only three eighth of the width (54 mm). The piece is already out of any structural grade. But the grain associated with the knot extends out 100mm and then it runs into a gum pocket. If you argue that the clear knot is what should be measured then the grader has to bring in another rule of sloping grain which again rules this defect piece out. The defect should have been docked out and the piece sold as two short lengths.

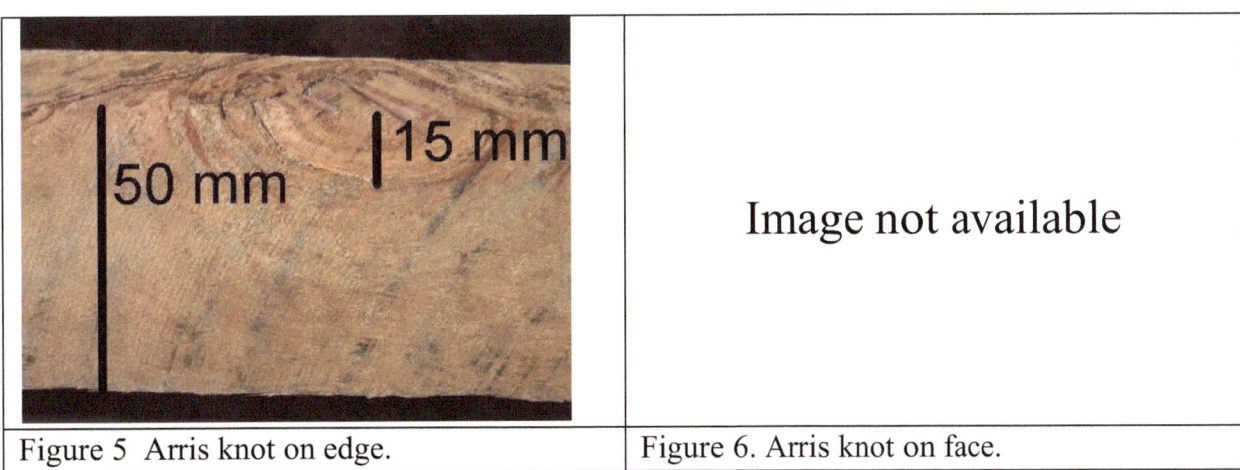

| Figure 5 Arris knot on edge. | Figure 6. Arris knot on face. |

The two knots on the arris are treated differently. In Figure 5 the longest dimension of the knot is on the face and the shorter measurement, 15 mm is on the edge. The measurement in this case is taken on the edge. This knot covers 30% of the face which meets the requirements of Structural Grade 3, or producing F14 in spotted gum.

I would assess this arris knot differently as the piece is serviceable and attempt to bring the piece into grade. This could include:

- Mentally removing any oversize amount say 3 mm from the defect.
- If the timber taken up by the knot was completely missing it would be then classed as "want and wane" (see below). The piece would have then passed Structural Grade 2 or F17.
- If this piece of timber was being dressed, an experienced operator could place the arris knot up as it went through the planer, removing 3 mm of material upgrading the timber to F17.[29]

In Figure 6 the arris knot extends the full width of the edge. It is measured on the face, not the edge.

| Figure 7. Knot with gum pocket. | Figure 8. Knot with shake. |

Knots are frequently associated with other defects. Figure 7 shows a knot associated with a gum pocket and is called an "encased knot". A less common knot is shown in Figure 8 where the knot is in association with a shake. The knot is measured to the furthest extremity of the combination defect. The boards in Figures 7 and 8 were within 300 mm of each other in adjacent boards. It is impossible for this deck to carry the design load in this area as both faults are too large to meet the requirements of Structural Grade 4, the lowest grade conceived. This illustrates the importance of getting the grading right at the mill as you cannot count on the builder to care/know and regrade. These defects would have been clearly evident at the time of laying. Figure 7 further illustrates the importance of going beyond AS2082 and grade for application. If the knot had been smaller so the timber did meet a structural grade the piece of timber would still have been unsuitable as the gum pocket, level with surface when first cut would be known to eventually wash out, as it has here, and produce a hazard for high heels.

---

[29] This assumes the timber is full size at 50 mm, 2 mm is removed from the bottom and 3mm from the top, finishing at 45mm.

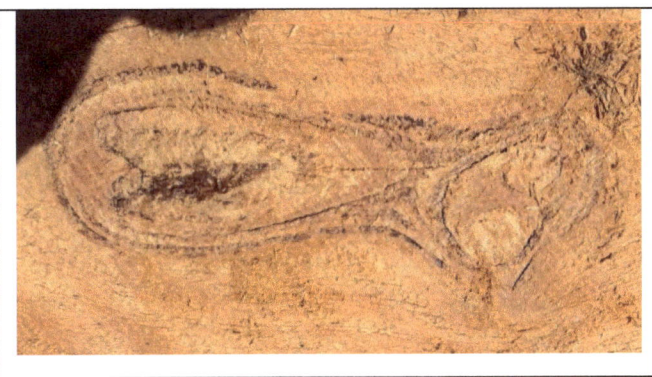	
Figure 9. Knot group.	Figure 10. Multiple knots.

Occasionally knots can come in groups and you simply measure across them at the widest point as in Figure 9. What is more complicated is when there are two unrelated knots close to each other. The grader is to measure longitudinally, not diagonally, between the knots. To be considered as separate knots, the distance must be two times the face width.[30] If the distance is less than two widths apart combine the total width of the two knots and then assess them as one knot. The image shown in Figure 10 is out of grade.

The pine Standard assesses knots differently to hardwood. There we have Knot area Ratio (KAR) defined as "The ration of the projected cross-sectional area of one or more knots to the cross-sectional area of the piece"[31] Basically, the grader had to look at both sides and average the size of the knot. This different approach is essential as knots are a far bigger problem with pine than with hardwood. For instance a 150 mm face with a 50 mm knot on one side and not visible on the other would be assessed as a 25 mm knot in pine but in hardwood it would be a 50 mm knot. In unseasoned spotted gum the piece would be graded as F11. If the practice of averaging was adopted the same piece would be graded as F17. A major review of the timber grading was undertaken in Queensland in 2003 with a view to introducing new grades and grading rules. It determined that KAR was equally appropriate for grading hardwood as well.[32] This means that a considerable amount of hardwood is being under-utilised and sold at a lower price than could otherwise be achieved.

---

[30] AS2082-2007 1.9.2.
[31] *AS 2858-2008 Timber - Softwood - Visually graded for structural purposes.*
[32] Department of Primary Industries. *Structural Hardwood Grading - Maximising the Potential of Structural Hardwoods Through Improved Knowledge of Characteristic Properties – Summary Report.* (Department of Primary Industries: Brisbane, 2003) 24.

Borer holes

Figure 11. Damage typical of the longicorn beetle.

Figure 12. Pinhole larvae holes.

When the highest grade of structural timber allows 12 borer holes up to 3 mm wide for a 100x100 mm area or equivalent, it is rare for this ever to be an issue. For F17 red ironbark (Structural Grade 3) the number of holes is unlimited and 20 are permitted in F17 spotted gum. When the hole size is larger than 3 mm they are graded as knots and two diameters is the required distance between the holes.

When used internally as say in a dressed exposed beam some distance from the eye, they present little issue as some well colour matched filler tales care of the aesthetics. Their presence in decking should be very limited as when used externally they fill with water and can cause degrade.

Termite Galleries

Figure 13. Termite Gallery on face and edge.

Figure 14. Termite gallery on face.

The grading of termite galleries in AS2086-1979 was that they were not permitted at all in Structural Grade 1 and for other grades they were treated as rot which was "surface and slight"[33] since the 2000 edition if the termite galleries are fully enclosed they are not permitted but if open for inspection they

---

[33] AS2083-1979 Clauses 1.1.2 (k) and 2,1,2 (k).

are classed as want and wane.[34] This is a better definition. The termite galleries in Figure 13 can be seen to only cover a part of the face and its extent down the side was visible at the time of grading. If this timber was totally removed it would pass the want and wane rule which will be described later. Again, while it might be suitable for some applications such as roof trusses it would not be suitable for decking.

Figure 15. Bad termite attack.

Figure 14 shows a termite gallery on the face only. There is no way of knowing if the activity is surface only or deep. Without probing it, which a grader does not have time to do; this defect should be docked out. In this particular piece there were two more patches of termite activity so the whole piece should have gone to the chipper. What is seen in Figure 15 could be just under the surface

Slope of Grain

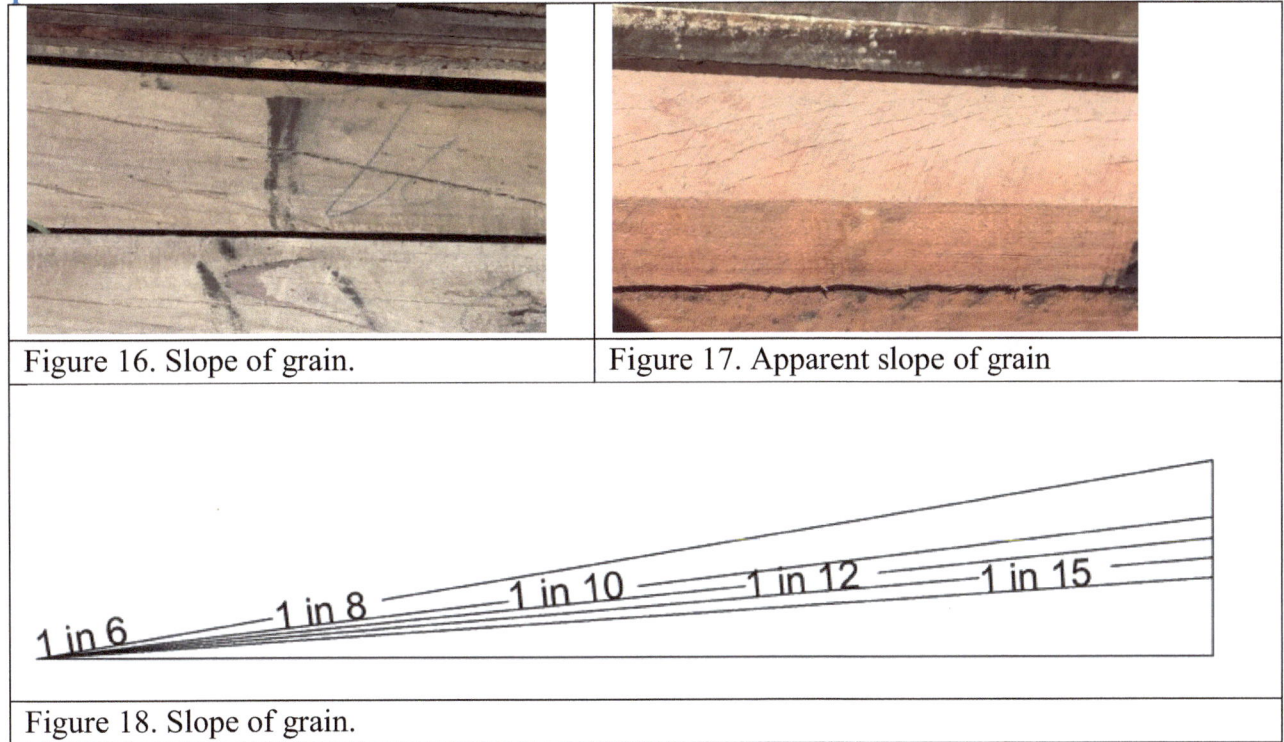

Figure 16. Slope of grain. Figure 17. Apparent slope of grain

Figure 18. Slope of grain.

When the grain is not straight the timber has a distinct loss of strength and in Figure 16 the timber is starting to separate down the sloping grain. Jarrah has proved to be more susceptible to the effects of

---

[34] AS2082-2000 Clause 2.1.1 (c).

sloping grain and has a much tighter than with the eastern Australian timbers, e.g. for Structural Grade 2 for all other species the allowance is 1 in 10 but for jarrah it is only 1 in 8, the allowance for Structural Grade 3.

Generally sloping grain around a knot is disregarded unless it significantly affects the general slope over half the width of the piece. In Figure 4 the grain of the timber slopes around the large knot and it would be out of grade on that account only. Sometimes the slope of grain is localised and when it does not extend over more than half the face it is ignored.

In Figure 17, after grading the timber has started to season and shallow checks have developed but they are sloping suggesting that the underlying grain is sloping. But it is not. Don't rush to judgment.

Heart

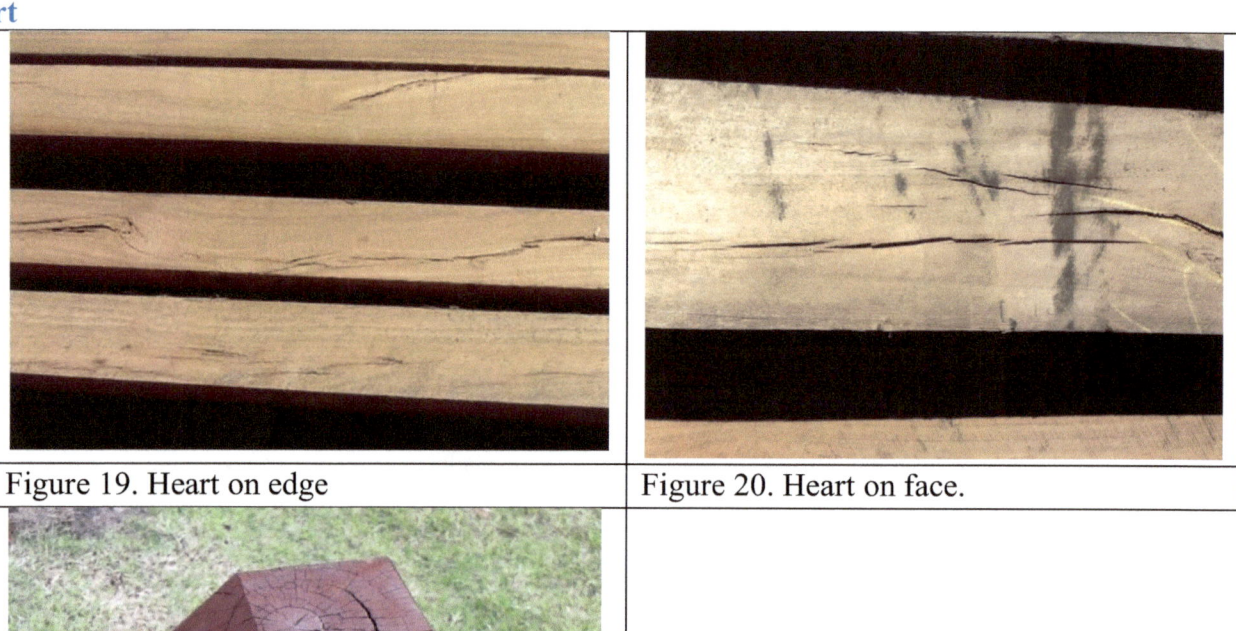

Figure 19. Heart on edge

Figure 20. Heart on face.

Figure 21. Heart in centre.

Heart is the most difficult part of sawn timber to grade, especially when it comes to grading for fitness for purpose. Unlike pine or cypress, the heart (or pith) of Australian Hardwood is not structural which is why it is necessary to restrict its use. AS2082 is not a great deal of help with grading of heart when comes to grading for fitness for purpose. It is too restrictive when considering heart on the face and edge and too generous regarding heart in the centre. This section deals only with heart on the edge and the face. For heart checks see Checks below. Heart in the centre is very complex and is covered separately under my discussion of 1.4.4 of AS2082-2007.

The basic requirement is that heart is not permitted where the smallest size is under 175 mm. The wording is proscriptive – **No heart** unlike say rot and termite galleries that are allowed to be, in effect, surface and slight. This is not reasonable and in reality is not what is regularly supplied. It would be rare to find even in a batch of high quality timber some 75 mm members that do not contain some heart. This is becoming more of a problem with the log size becoming smaller. The standard does not differentiate between a 38, 50 or 75 mm thick member where the effect of heart is increasingly less. When we developed Joistwood we tested 150x75 mm with slight heart, because that was what was being supplied, and found it had no trouble meeting the structural requirements of F17.

Figure. 22. This 250x100 is strictly out of grade.

Figure 22 shows a 250x100 mm bearer which is 6.6 m long. Few logs will produce this size timber so it is a very hard piece to cut. To reject this piece because there was a touch of heart on one end would be a very poor and irresponsible use of a limited resource. How can you sympathetically grade this piece? Firstly, it was 1mm oversize so with the undersize allowance you can mentally take off 4mm from face with heart. If there was an internal check with associated shelling out you would allow a further 10% of the cross section to be completely missing. The heart has now, mentally at least, disappeared. So, I would pass this piece despite the literal wording of AS2082.

A 75 mm structural member will carry some heart on its face. The grader can check the growth rings at both ends to see where the heart would be. If the ends are free of heart and the heart looks slight you can be assured that the heart is slight. He/she can further put a tape measure on the width, if it is full size, you can mentally take off the sawing tolerance, the effect of heart is reduced, and then you can mentally take off the want and wane (explained later) and the piece of timber is as acceptable for a structural purpose as a piece totally free of heart. Graders need to use some common sense[35] when it comes to heart in larger sizes as some of these larger sizes are extremely hard to cut and should not be rejected without a valid reason.

As a dressed decorative piece at eye level heart is not acceptable, as a simple structural member it can be accepted when slight on 75 mm or larger members. Heart should probably be limited on the edges.

---

[35] An oxymoron as it describes something that is increasingly uncommon.

Gum veins

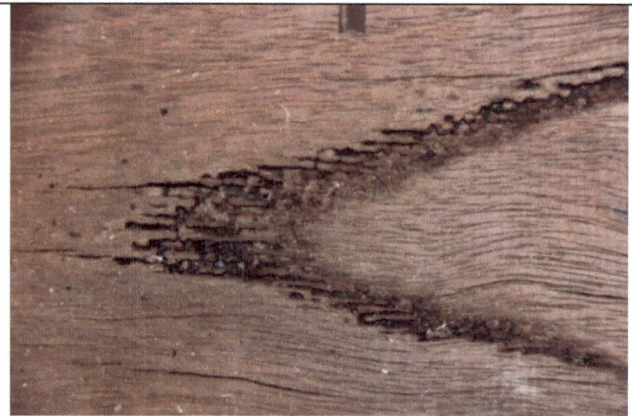 Figure 23. Tight gum vein Image Gary Hopewell	Figure 24. Loose gum vein
 Figure 25. The extreme effect of a loose gum vein.	 Figure 26. Boards with gum vein.

A common natural defect is gum veins. They can look very unsightly as figure 26 shows but often it does not have any real structural effect. Gum veins are either tight, i.e. they have interconnecting tissue between both sides of the vein as in Figure 23. The allowance for tight gum veins is generous and with the allowance in Structural Grade 1 being up to one and a half times the length in aggregate, these pieces are very likely in grade providing there is interconnecting tissue. They would be very unsuitable for decking as they will delaminate in time leaving dangerous splinters.

The feature in Figure 25 is described as "shelling out". Here there is a loose gum vein but sometimes there are two distinct sections without any gum between them. It would then be classed as a heart shake – see "Shakes" below.

Gum, Latex, Resin Pockets

Figure 27. Measuring gum veins.

Figure 28. Gum vein intersecting an edge.

Gum pockets are measured radially (Figure 27), that is to say, not the distance across the face but the depth, measured from the top face into the timber with the ruler aligned at a 90 degree to the internal face. So the defect could be quite wide across the face but the measurement given to the defect could be relatively small. The gum vein in Figure 27 measures 10 mm. The highest grade, Structural Grade 1, allows the lesser of up a quarter of the width of the surface or 12 mm.

Gum pockets frequently intersect two surfaces (Figure 28) and in these cases the permissible measurement is reduced. For Structural Grade 1 the measurement is halved.

Figure 29. Gum pocket in decking.

The allowance under AS2082 is very generous but despite that no gum pockets are acceptable in decking as splinters can develop from them

End Splits

Figure 30. Single end split.

Figure 31. Multiple end split.

End splits are ones that extend from face to face as in Figure 30 and can be either single or multiple. In Figure 31 there are end splits and checks which do not go from face to face. The checks are not included in the measurement. When the grader assesses a multiple end split he/she is required to measure all the splits to come to his assessment, not just the longest. The split in Figure 30 is not allowed in structural timber but this piece is a landscaping sleeper which has no structural grade. This lower, non structural grade is why professional designers should never use the word "sleeper" in their specification.[36]

When the split is not the same length on both faces, the shortest length is measured as the length of the split and the remaining length on one side is classed as a check – see below.

Where AS2082 gives no guidance is what to do when a piece is over length. Say the length ordered by the customer is 3.6 m and the piece cut is actually 3.7 m. If the end split is 200 mm long the piece, otherwise without defect, is out of grade for all Strength Groups. But then the timber is going to be trimmed back 100mm making the effective split 100 mm bringing it back into grade for all Groups. The prevailing thought is that best practice for freshly cut timber ideally should be supplied with the split in as freshly cut timber can continue to split after defect docking.

Preferably over length timber should be supplied but with a docking mark that forces the builder to trim as required (but with the standard of some builders that can be risky). Practice from larger mills is to use automated dockers and produce uniform length packs being 50 to 100 mm over-length which have better retail presentation but possibly not best practice.

---

[36] Refer to my book, *The Seven Deadly Sins of Timber Design*.

Checks

Figure 32. Surface checks. Figure 33. Surface checks.

The allowance for surface checks is generous. Even in the highest grade, Structural Grade 1, a check is allowed up to ¼ of the length and 3 mm wide. Checks intersecting an end and an end split should not be confused. If the crack does not go from face to face it is not an end split (refer Figure 31). The check is measured across the face.

Figure 34. Internal check.

The checks shown in Figures 32 and 33 are due to seasoning. Sometimes there is a void in the timber, either totally enclosed as in Figure 34 or exposed during sawing. The combined cross section of an internal check cannot exceed 10% for all grades

Shakes

Figure 35. Heart shake. Figure 36. Cross shake.

There is a note not to confuse checks with shakes[37]. Figure C6 of AS2082 shows three different types of shakes but mentions five in the definitions.

- Heart
- Star
- Ring (or water) and
- Cross.
- Radial

While a check can look similar to a heart shake, the difference is that a check runs from the outside in towards the centre whereas the heart shake runs from the centre towards the outside as shown in Figure 35. The presence of a heart shake indicates low strength material. When the heart is in the centre these shakes can radiate outwards in a star pattern (Figure 37).

Figure 37. Star shake in recycled timber.

Figure 38. Ring shake.

Figure 39. Radial shake

Figure 38 shows a ring or water shake. Figure 25 shows an extreme gum vein which can give the same effect that results when this timber is sawn, a concave section is completely missing. There appears to be no guidance in AS2082 as to how to grade this. I would assess this similarly to a check which would only be in grade if no more than 10% of the cross section is missing (in all grades).

Occasionally there are fractures running crosswise. The check in Figure 36 was so large that the piece broke into two pieces. These cross shakes are not allowed. In the grading rules cross shakes come under the General section of each grade description [38] where they are called "compression failures".

---

[37] AS2082-2007 C5.
[38] AS2082-2007 2.1.1, 2.2.1, 2.3.1, 2.4.1.

Radial shakes (Figure 39) can develop in logs that sit in the mill yard for too long before cutting.

Rot

| Figure 40. Rot. | Figure 41. Fruiting bodies |

All grades have the same requirements for rot; no more than 3 mm deep and not covering more than 150 x 100 mm. Rot is distinguished by its different texture. The rot shown in Figure 40 is out of grade. Figure 41 shows white fruiting bodies which contain fungal spores. This means that the timber is infected despite the timber still feeling and looking sound. If used in a location that is permanently dry decay is not likely to progress but a producer does not have this control. This material should be docked.

Figure 42. Surface mould on Tanalith E treated timber.

The white fruiting bodies in Figures 40 and 41 indicate that the decay present in the timber is not the same as the virtually identical appearance that can develop during warm humid conditions on timber treated with Tanalith E and ACQ (Figure 42). This mould does not penetrate the surface of the timber and can be easily washed or brushed off. Treatment of the Work Tank solution with a proprietary mouldicide should be a standard practice at all of the treatment plants where conditions may encourage the growth of moulds

The Standard requires the person to judge primary rot, not any subsequent decay.

Want and Wane

Figure 43. Want and wane, note included bark.

Figure 44. Forklift damage.

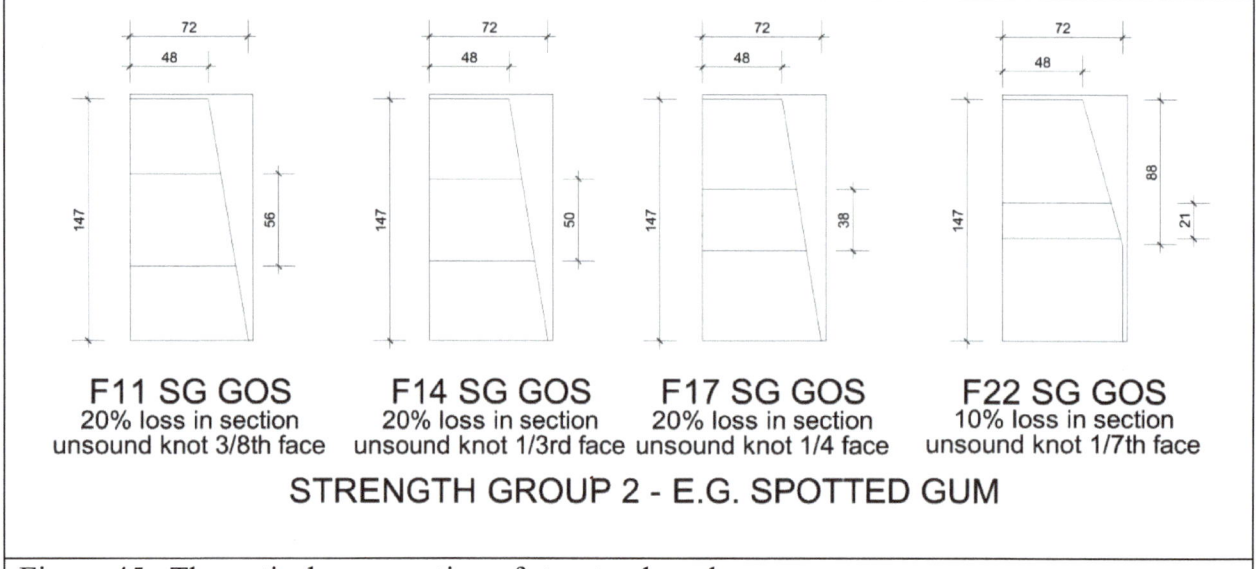

Figure 45. Theoretical cross section of structural grades.

We have discussed various defects but it needs to be understood that these defects can exist in conjunction with other defects. Figure 45 shows the theoretical cross section of 150x75 mm spotted gum (SG) for Structural Grade 4 (F11 SG GOS[39]) through to Structural Grade 1 (F22 SG GOS). The drawing shows first the sawing tolerance loss of 3 mm, then the knot which can be unsound, i.e. no better than a hole and then loss of section due to want and wane. The allowance is generous.

Forklift damage, a common enough problem, should be assessed as want and wane.

---

[39] GOS is industry abbreviation for green off saw.

Lyctus Susceptible Sapwood

| Fig. 46. Lyctus Damage. Image courtesy South Coast Home Check. | Fig. 47. Lyctus larvae. Image courtesy of Doug Howick. |

The standard only refers to lyctus susceptible sapwood. The sapwood of some species contains starch which makes them susceptible to attack by the larvae of the lyctus beetle. These larvae will turn this sapwood to powder. Tables A1 to A4 list the lyctus susceptibility or otherwise of common species. Both New South Wales and Queensland had excellent legislation preventing the sale of untreated susceptible sapwood but tragically both acts have been repealed.[40]

A specifier should not allow untreated lyctus susceptible sapwood to be used irrespective of the 10 percent allowance in Structural Grade 1 as it will turn to powder. Imagine the damage done in Figure 44 should it be within the allowable percentage but part of an exposed architectural truss.

Fig. 48. Blackbutt sapwood is not attacked by lyctus.

In Figure 48 we see a 50 mm thick flitch of blackbutt with sapwood on both edges. The timber cut from it will invariably contain some sapwood. There is no restriction in the amount of sapwood which can occur in non lyctus susceptible timber. This sapwood does not contain starch so if it is used internally in an internal architectural truss there are no problems as the sapwood will not degrade and there will be no lyctus attack. This same piece, if used externally, externally, where it is exposed to moisture, the sapwood will decay and at the very least look unsightly. The sapwood of non susceptible timber should also be treated if being used externally.

---

[40] Queensland in 2010 and NSW in 2013.

Straightness

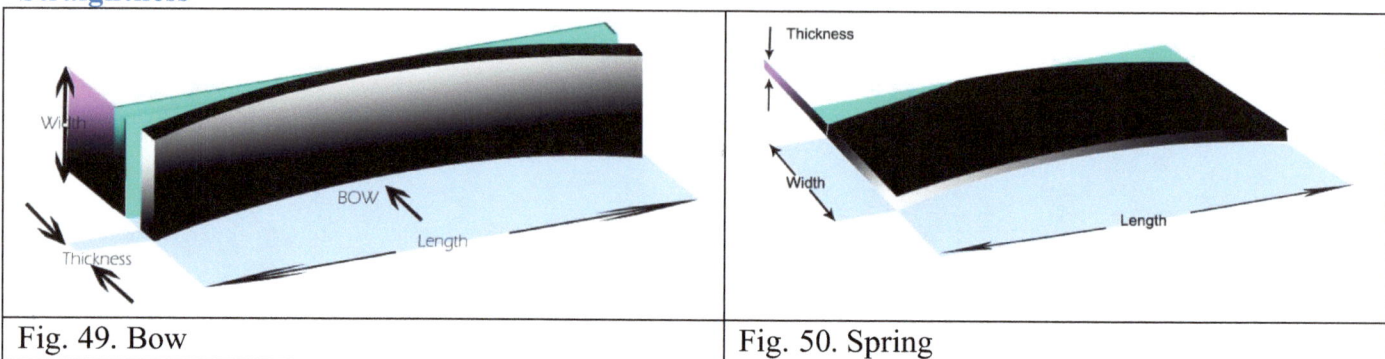

Fig. 49. Bow   Fig. 50. Spring

Builders will forgive almost any defect except straightness. This, more than anything, impacts upon the speed of construction and the profitability of the contract. Timber can be out of straight in two ways, it can contain either bow or spring (and sometimes both). Figures 49 and 50 illustrate the difference. The amount of bow and spring allowed is again very generous and the permissible limits are given in Table C1 of AS2082-2007. The Standard's perception of its allowance for bow and spring is that it is conservative. Despite the purpose of the standard being to allow timber to be graded for structural purposes[41] the bow and spring allowance is described as follows:

The limits of bow, spring and twist in this Standard are based on utility considerations, which are more conservative than structural considerations.[42]

When AS2082 was first introduced in 1977 many smaller producers, who took pride in the straightness of their timber, saw the standard as representing a lowest common denominator approach, accommodating the larger mills. They generally had a lower standard for straightness. In earlier days millers used to make straightening cuts to ensure these larger sizes were straight as they came from the mill. Modern sawing practices in large mills seldom allow this. Instead it is intended to produce one product per pass through the saw bench.

A 200x75 bearer at 8.4m long was initially allowed 55 mm for both bow and spring. Later standards (2000 and 2007) reduced the amount of bow and spring for longer lengths. The maximum now allowed for a 200mm piece is 40 mm.

Modern milling practices are such that, if structural timber is not straight, it should only contain bow, not spring. It is much easier to push a 50 mm thick member sideways by 50 mm to straighten it than it is to pull that member down by 50 mm. With items such as floor joists which are 38 and 50 mm, bow within the permissible standards of AS2082 - 2007 is only an annoyance but not so when the members are 75 mm or larger. At this thickness the member becomes extremely stiff and is very hard to straighten.[43] When the standard is reviewed, serious consideration should be given to reducing the measurements for thicker members.

---

[41] AS2082-2007 1.1.
[42] AS2082-2007 1.7.3 Note.
[43] I recall having an upset builder return a large bearer to me. Its straightness was within the limits of AS2082 but when he tried to straighten it on site freshly laid bricks on a pillar broke off.

Studs and lintels have to be straight and the changes introduced in the 1979 Standard recognized this and introduced these as formal grades with more stringent tables for straightness.[44] For instance, a 2.4 m stud could have 6 mm spring (the noggings straightened any bow). By comparison, a 75x50 mm structural piece is allowed 12 mm, twice the amount. It is simply not possible to build to an acceptable standard with studs that have 12 mm spring. It was not uncommon to see a hardwood stud cut almost in half in an attempt to straighten it.[45] These important grades were discontinued in 2000 revision. In its place was inserted Clause 1.7.3 which said special arrangements can be made between buyer and seller to limit the amount of bow, spring and twist for certain products. I have never seen this done.

An important part of the standard relating to straightness is the instruction to measure bow and spring against a straight-line (generally a tape measure in practice) held at both ends.[46]

Fig. 51. Checking a bearer for bow.

Appearance Grades

The four structural grades are available in what are called Structural Appearance Grades and their definition is found in Section 2.5. These grades are based on the structural grades e.g. a 150x50 mm appearance grade spotted gum in F14 still has a knot a third of the face or 50 mm across (and you could question how "appearance grade" that is) but the knot now has to be solid. There is a blanket prohibition on defects such as decay and want and wane.

Keeping to the example of a 150x50 mm spotted gum, F17 and F22 in appearance grade is starting to look like a reasonable piece of timber but is not suitable for all applications such as handrail.[47] Specifying a structural appearance grade is no guarantee that the timber received will meet expectation, particularly when it comes to included heart. Ultimately, with appearance grade timber, the acceptability of a piece of timber for an appearance application is very much in the eye of the beholder. One client expects nothing short of perfection while another is ecstatic with a piece of low quality recycled timber.

---

[44] AS2082-1979 Clauses 2.5 and 2.6.
[45] A practice so common it had its own term "Crippling".
[46] See Appendix 2 for a personal reflection on measuring straightness.
[47] See Chapter 3, Specifying timber handrail.

Durability, the Great Omission

As you read through this book you will develop an understanding of timber grading and the effect of different types of "natural characteristics", a euphemism for the emotive term, "defect". You will be able to read and apply AS2082 with greater understanding. However understanding what a standard, that is fundamentally limited, says is inadequate until we understand what it does not say. Its great omission is durability. In the 1979 standard designers are advised to abandon the previous terminology and now order by F rating[48]. These specifications frequently had durability at the forefront and must be reintroduced in some form when the primary consideration is exposure to the elements.

Many readers would be aware of a much publicised fatal deck collapse in Hamilton in Brisbane in 2008. There had been an error in construction 85 years previously which led to this loss of life. The point I am trying to make is that the timber was 85 years old and it was construction practices that caused the problem, not the durability of the timber. I would have expected the Hamilton timber to have been originally ordered as "Royal Species", a term I will shortly describe, or one of that group of species mentioned by name.

Figure 52. F17 Timber joist failed after 3 ½ years.

Against the durability that could be achieved before the introduction of F ratings, consider the joist in Figure 1 which was specified as F17 and nothing more. It had failed after three and a half years. I was called in to confirm that the timber was indeed F17 but being Victorian ash it was never an appropriate timber to use in that application due to its low durability, irrespective of its strength. That species when used externally can regularly fail at between 3 to 5 years depending on circumstances.

There was a simple term that was used when durable timber was required. It would be ordered as "royal

---

[48] AS2082-1979 Preface.

species". This has been defined as "A collection of eucalypt timbers which command a premium in price because of their great durability and strength".[49] But what constitutes this collection? I have met people who claim to have a seen a definitive list but no one has been able to point me to a document where it can actually be found. Until I can find such a list, the prevailing and probably correct view is that this was a marketing term adopted by the industry. An old (90 years plus) senior forester recalled it this way:

There were two lists; one was decorative and covered cabinet timber such as silky oak, cedar, walnut and beach. (I personally have never heard it used this way so it must have fallen out of use a long time ago). The second list was for structural timber and included the species gray and red ironbark, spotted gum, tallowwood, and yellow stringybark. To be a royal species the timber had to be:

- Readily available
- Extractable, and
- Have a ready market.

The list varied from state to state and in Western Australia included jarrah and karri despite being of lower durability than the eastern Australian list.[50]

Species	Strength Group	Durability (In ground)	Shrinkage (tangential)
Brush Box	3	3	9.7%
Red Mahogany	2	2	6.3%
Sydney Blue Gum	3	3	9.5%
Gray Ironbark	1	1	7.5%
Blackbutt	2	2	7.3%
Bloodwood	3	1	4.0%
Grey gum	1	1	7.0%
Table 3. Timbers claimed to be "royal species".[51] Only gray ironbark actually is.			

Unfortunately, this very useful specification has now been "corrupted"[52] by an industry which seeks a marketing advantage at the expense of losing the certainty that was previously ensured. Now almost anything seems to be claimed to be a "royal species" regardless of performance and properties. Table Three shows species claimed to be royal species as found in sales information of two New South Wales timber manufacturers. Only one of these actually is, grey ironbark. When timbers with such diverse properties are lumped together and called "very hard and durable" it seems obvious that the term "royal species" is in the process of being devalued to the point of being useless. While I have not observed this inclusive use of the term with Queensland suppliers, the damage is done.

So, with a very good term being taken from us, where does a specifier turn when they want to ensure timber, not just with sufficient strength but with the necessary durability is supplied? Outdoor Structures Australia developed, tested and engineered two proprietary products, Deckwood and

---

[49] Anonymous. *Dictionary of Timber Terms* (Timber Secretarial Group: Sydney U.D.)
[50] *Pers. Com.* Walter Smith. Jan 18, 2013.
[51] Tait Flooring. URL http://www.taitflooring.com.au/pages/products/flooring/timber-types/royal-species.php. Date accessed 5 August 2013, MCM Hardwood. URL http://www.infolink.com.au/c/MCM-Hardwood. Date accessed 5 August 2013,
[52] "Corrupted" is not as strong a word as I would have liked to use as it implies ignorance. "Bastardised", with its connotation of a deliberate seems more appropriate but modesty prevails.

Joistwood with full design information that demystified the specification of weather exposed timber. It left the designers free to do what they did well and as for what had not been done well, we simply took care of that in the background. Some designers trusted themselves to these products and reported very good results. Others took a high ground stance and said "We will not use a proprietary product" pointing to corporate policy demanding only Australian Standard product be used. Our design guides would then be ignored, not differentiating the best practice design outlined in the guides from the best practice product. This would perpetuate standard practice which, only too often, was bad practice. It was hard to feel sympathy when these jobs failed prematurely but, as a supplier, we could not distance ourselves from them. Each bad experience meant one less customer for timber and this ultimately impacted on my own business.

So where do you go when durability is the prime consideration and you are specifying with a standard that ignores your primary consideration? Deckwood and Joistwood which was tested and proven was the obvious answer but if they are ruled out by specifiers then I really do not know. We are involved with an industry that will try to push whatever species is available to the miller/reseller. We also have an industry that will supply you whatever you ask, whether it is suitable or not.

You may well say to me that "We have Durability Classes to guide us. If a timber is Durability Class 2 it will be serviceable". If I suggested what about specifying Durability Class 3 instead you would correctly tell me I am being irresponsible. But what about a durability Class 2 timber that has only just tipped over the border from being a high Durability 3 to being a low Durability 2 as compared to another timber that may be Durability 2 and almost a Durability 1? These two timbers will perform very differently in extreme situations. How does a specifier know which is which? He doesn't! This was the strength of the "royal species" terminology. An example of this difference is blackbutt. It is Durability 2 in ground but Durability 1 above ground which is the same as spotted gum. But Queensland bridge specifications will only allow blackbutt in the deck where it is protected by a bitumen running surface whereas spotted gum can be used in the harder to replace members such as girders and headstocks. Blackbutt is not allowed at all in Queensland as railway sleepers nor as crossarms in the power distribution industry, yet again, spotted gum can be used in these applications. A specifier looking at standards and not aware of the broader industry experience would not make any effort to exclude blackbutt and promote spotted gum or other royal species.

There is a real need to develop a simple terminology for a defined group of high performing timbers. The industry and designers can take hold of this terminology in their specification and be prepared to pay for the certainty that comes with some species. In its absence, the advice of the old forester is still sound. We would add a few extra species for certain applications. As an example, forest red gum is In Ground Durability 1 and we would use it without hesitation as a boardwalk joist but it makes poor decking and as a bollard the tops tend to split. The royal species list did not need this type of qualification.

The opinion of old experienced millers is that AS2082 needs a very clear statement that timber specified by F ratings alone may be very inappropriate for many applications.

Chapter 2. Section 1 of AS2082

Some aspects of Section 1 of AS2082 are not straightforward and this chapter amplifies those areas that experience has shown needs some explanation.

1.1.2 Scope and Application of AS2082

Many of my readers would recall the pine industry transitioning from F grades to a designation starting with MGP (machine graded pine). Large pine mills no longer grade by visual inspection but have very expensive machines that "stress grade" every piece of structural timber that passes through the production line. By measuring the deflection of each piece under a given load, its grade is easily determined. However the expense involved with the purchase and maintenance of such machinery, let alone the fact that they would have to be far larger, is out of the reach of all but the very largest hardwood mill, even if such machinery even existed.

AS2082 provides a hardwood producer with a low cost and very simple means of supplying hardwood at a nominated stress grade for structural purposes. When the Standard was released in 1977 it was generally[53] welcomed as it brought together in one place a number of previous Australian and industry standards. It was for all that a flawed document and it was revised in 1979, 2000 and 2010. The preface to all these revision cite, among other reasons for changes being the need to "correct some errors and anomalies". This reflects the difficulty bringing together one standard that addresses the over 200 species of hardwoods milled commercially (all behaving slightly differently), the wide variety of defects experienced and the range of different applications. Pressures from industry also have an impact on changes. My own Deckwood standard has undergone five revisions in 15 years and it is a single product, limited species specification.

The Standard provides a very valuable, but limited tool for the many small hardwood mills scattered throughout the nation. It allows someone who has completed a fairly simple and short course in grading to be able to place a tape measure over a natural feature in any piece of hardwood and assess it according to the four grade descriptions in the Standard. From these grade descriptions the F grade can be determined. The grade descriptions also allow someone else to apply the same rules and confirm the grade. Grading was no longer arbitrary. There should be no more than 5% disagreement and then only by one grade. The complication for any confirmation grade is that the grader does not grade what is seen before him but what he imagines the timber was like on the day of milling/processing.

| Fig. 53. Roof trusses, one structural application. | Fig. 54. Weather exposed decks, a totally different structural application. |

---

[53] Not universally, it was seen by some as a lowering of their standards.

This is another weakness of AS2082. Knowing the strength properties on the day of milling/processing often is not enough. You have already read my thoughts of the Great Omission of durability from the standard but there are also many other factors to consider. The Scope covers timber used "for structural purposes" but is that for **all** structural purposes? A roof truss is as simple an application as can be found. After placement, the roof goes on and then a ceiling so the timber never sees a critical eye, a drop of water or any UV. Shrinkage is not even much of an issue as everything indexes from the bottom of the truss which is basically constant. All that is needed is to know its strength[54] and knowing how well the timber holds the nail plate. The boardwalk however has different requirements which are:

- The timber has to look good
- Splinters are an issue
- The timber must be able to resist UV and moisture
- Shrinkage can cause large gaps and endanger the public
- The timber must be stable
- The timber must be termite resistant
- The timber must not burn easily
- The timber must be durable

Though some guidance is given in AS2082 as to appearance (not adequately for all circumstances as will be demonstrated), do not look to this standard if you want help with the critical properties for weather exposed timber. Despite the very different requirements for the timber in these two applications, generally we see the same specification for both, F14 or F17 and no (or little) more. That is when we see a specification at all! Some designers are still just saying "hardwood decking".

When I first started selling hardware all our bolts were black steel with no corrosion protection at all. Tables existed that gave the structural properties of these bolts. They worked very well under a roof but would you use them to build a wharf on the coast? The idea is preposterous as corrosion resistance is the primary property to be resolved, and no amount of design information on black bolts will cause you to even consider them. Known strength on the day of installation is fundamentally useless information, nothing but stainless will do. Likewise, knowing the properties on the day of milling/processing is no guide to a piece of timber's properties after 20 years in the weather. Specifying only by F ratings is just the same as asking for black steel bolts. The more so when very few understand what these F ratings represent.

Unfortunately, with little formal training being given in timber at universities few professionals have the knowledge to write a specification that is the timber equivalent to a stainless steel bolt. It was for just this reason that my company introduced Deckwood and Joistwood to the market. By just nominating these products we took care of all of this for you? What follows will give a good understanding of why such a specification, or a highly qualified variation to AS 2082, is necessary.

1.3 Referenced Documents
There are five Australian Standards and seven Australian/New Zealand Standards referenced. Four of these need comment.

AS2878 Timber - Classification into strength groups
At the core of AS2082 is another standard AS2878 Timber - Classification into strength groups. The background for this classification has been outlined in Chapter 1. After testing samples that are free of

---

[54] Strength usually governs over stiffness with roof trusses.

any natural feature and sourced from different locations, each species is allocated into one of seven strength groups for unseasoned timber and eight for seasoned. The properties of each group are tabled below. It is important to understand that these values do not represent commercially available grades and sizes in real life situations.

Minimum values (MPa) for green timber							
Strength Property	S1	S2	S3	S4	S5	S6	S7
MOR	103	86	73	62	52	43	36
MOE	16300	14200	12400	10700	9100	7900	6900
MCS	52	43	36	31	26	22	18
Minimum values (MPa) for seasoned timber							
Strength Property	SD1	SD2	SD3	SD4	SD5	SD6	SD7	SD8
MOR	150	130	110	94	78	65	55	45
MOE	21500	18500	16000	14000	12500	10500	9100	7900
MCS	80	70	61	54	47	41	36	30
Table 4. Properties of different strength groups. 55								

There is a wide range of the MOE varying from 6900 to 21500 MPa, a threefold difference, Durability is even more varied but is not considered in AS 2082. Castrol ran a very successful add campaign for years based on the slogan, "Oils ain't oils". The same is even more so with timber.

AS1604.1 Specification for preservative treatment
In my guide to timber preservation I wrote in detail about the false sense of security that AS1604.1 engenders. Basically you can only treat sapwood with commercial treatments. As most sawn structural members contain little sapwood and as the rules for want and wane (and forklift damage) we have learnt are extremely generous, it makes little structural difference in larger sizes whether the sapwood decays or not. AS2082 is primarily about structural issues, not aesthetics.

Apart from smaller members such as domestic decking, invariably there is not enough sapwood to anguish over whether timber is H3 or H6. Yet some do just that and cause unnecessary complications such as introducing arsenic, chrome and creosote where there is no need. Correct specification of natural durability is more important than relying on preservation as your prime means of durability.

AS1148 Nomenclature - Australian, New Zealand and imported species
Nomenclature is the term given to a system of names used in a particular field. Is there a difficulty about naming trees? Yes there is, and it is an area where specifiers need to be extremely cautious. There are Standard Trade Names, formalised in AS 1148, local names and even marketing names. These local and marketing names can be very misleading[56], and sometimes intentionally misleading. Careful attention must be given to what you call certain species and what you exclude in the

---

[55] Forest Products Commission Western Australia. *Timber Advisory Notes*
http://www.fpc.wa.gov.au/content_migration/plantations/species/species_notes.aspx. date Accessed, 5 July 2012
[56] A good source of local names given against the botanical names and the trades can be found at
http://www.daff.qld.gov.au/26_5509.htm . Date accessed, 9 July 2012.

specification. In South East Queensland you will hear one species referred to in the industry as "blue gum" but its common trade name is "forest red gum". Over the border into New South Wales, "blue gum" refers to a species with the Common Trade name of Sydney blue gum. The timber sawn from both species is of a similar red colour but has widely different properties. This is not a theoretical problem. Consider this email about a timber deck along a foreshore.

> "Ted,
>
> I am writing to seek some advice regarding timber decking with relation to a project we have underway in xxx.
>
> The scenario is that the deck was specified as F17 spotted gum or grey ironbark hardwood. No mention of seasoned timber. But notes in the specification did include ''All decking shall be ordered at the commencement of the project and be suitably dried."
>
> Through various convoluted processes it ended up that we approved the contractors recommended alternative of 'Grey Gum'. I was advised at the time that Parks XXX used this timber for jetty decking. After further investigation I was told that the timber was in fact Mountain Grey Gum milled here in Victoria in the north/northwest region. The specification for it was still F17.
>
> As I understand it the timber was milled this time last year. At this stage I cannot confirm that. This information is based on the time of the approval and a discussion I had with the timber supplier. Subsequently the decking was laid from May last year to present. The boards were laid between 1 and 2 mm apart and screwed into place with 100 mm bugle batten screws.
>
> At this present moment the Client is ropeable due to the decking warping, cupping and spaces between boards being anywhere between 6 to 25 mm and screws being exposed by up to 8 mm. The specified maximum spacing was "6 mm at equilibrium moisture content" and the screws countersunk 3 mm.
>
> Can you please advise if the timber used would react so differently to the specified timber? Would standard practice for decking preparation be to cure it for a period of time? Has an incorrect timber been used for decking? ... I would greatly appreciate your professional and experienced opinion about this matter".

What the sawmiller did was unconscionable as you cannot simply be that ignorant of the material you produce for a living. Without looking up Bootle's *Wood in Australia* he would have known how it behaved. The text book says about mountain grey gum:

- The heartwood is said to only be moderately durable. It is only class 3 in ground whereas highly durable timbers are needed.
- It has high shrinkage (10% tangential)
- Collapse occurs during drying (ruling out a natural sawn low slip top surface)

- It should only be quarter-sawn to avoid surface checking which if severe impacts adversely on longevity and appearance, and;
- It is only suitable for general construction purposes, not specialised applications such as heavy engineering construction, which includes bridges and wharves. [57]

But by substituting a local for a common name and certifying to an F grade the mill still supplied it. Are you are going to award your order to the lowest price tenderer who may well be a brother of this miller? The matter gets even more complicated with marketing names as opposed to local and trade names, e.g. Pacific tallowwood, and Pacific jarrah.

Figure. 55. Pacific tallowwood (garo garo) after four years in north Queensland. Image courtesy Timber Queensland

Tallowwood is one of Australia's finest timbers as it is dense, durable and strong. It is a durability Class 1 timber both in and above ground. A kiln dried piece of tallowwood, suitable for decking, is rated as F34 By calling something Pacific tallowwood[58] immediately brings up the connotations of all that is good about tallowwood. But call it by its common trade name, garo garo, and you get an entirely different picture. Table Five compares the two species based on figures available at the time garo garo was first introduced to the Australian market.

trade name	Botanical name	Kg at 12° MC	Hardness	Strength group	Joint Group	In Ground Durability	Above Ground Durability	Shrinkage	Lyctus Susceptible	Termite Resistant
Tallowwood	*Eucalyptus microcorys*	1010	Very hard	S2	J1	1	1		Yes	Yes
Garo Garo[59]	*Mastixiodendron pachyclados*	700-935	Hard	S4	J3	2	2	High	?	No

Table 5. Comparison of tallowwood[60] with Pacific tallowwood

---

[57] Bootle, Keith R. *Wood in Australia, Types Properties and Uses, Second Edition*. (McGraw Hill: Sydney, 1983) 280.
[58] Refer to TLB Timber website http://tlbtimber.com.au/Timber%20Types%20and%20Grades.pdf Date accessed, 9 July 2012. There the joint group is also listed as J2, not J3
[59] Garo garo information sourced from Hopewell, G (ed.). *Construction timbers in Queensland: properties and specifications for satisfactory performance of construction timbers in Queensland - Class 1 and Class 10 buildings, books* 2. (Department of Primary Industries and Fisheries: Queensland. 2007) Note that the March 2013 edition downgraded Garo garo to In Gound and Above Ground Durability 4.
[60] Hopewell, *Construction 2...*, 63 and 75.

So it is clear that true Australian tallowwood and the garo garo sold under the marketing name of Pacific tallowwood, despite being of similar colour, are very different timbers in their performance. Later testing, following its poor performance in Australia saw the figures originally supplied from New Guinea drastically revised downwards. The species is now rated at Durability 4 In and Above Ground. Yet, on the basis of the original data alone it should never have been considered as a replacement for the highly durable Australian hardwoods.

Pacific jarrah is another marketing name which was first given to *Manilkara bidentata* (common name balata), a hardwood from South America. But here we have a timber that outperforms the original in landscaping items. My experience with it was very favourable[61] and better than that which you would expect from jarrah. It is harder, more durable, and more dense. Now this has become more complicated. The genus "Manilkara" is much like "Eucalyptus" in that it encompasses a wide range of species with different properties. It is different in that this genus grows naturally in a much wider range, in tropical and subtropical areas which include Africa, Madagascar, Asia, Australia and South America. At the time of writing Manilkara kanosiensis an endangered[62] Asian timber is being sold by different importers alongside the south American timber as Pacific Jarrah.

Your specification should be free of any reference to local names and to marketing names. It should either:

- refer to Outdoor Structures (or its licensee's) Deckwood and Joistwood,
- if piloting your own course among the minefield, reference *AS1148 Nomenclature - Australian, New Zealand and imported species* as the definition of the names of the species or.
- If not listed in AS 1148, use its botanical name.

Confirming the species you have specified

Specifying a species is well and good but how do you tell what you have? It is relatively easy to tell what species timber you are dealing with when you see a standing tree with its bark and leaves but sawn timber is a totally different matter. When freshly sawn, there can be very little colour difference separating species with very different performances. There is nothing separating them at all when it has all turned a uniform silver grey and the consequence of substitution is becoming obvious. When freshly sawn and treated there is no colour separation at all. A quick guide to help you identify what species you are actually dealing with is the burnt splinter test. While timber may burn, each species has a characteristic way of burning. The image above shows how effective and simple this test is. Table Six lists the burning splinter tests for a number of species.[63]

---

[61] My use was in heavy landscaping such as commercial fencing. I have had reports of the timber having a high unit shrinkage value making it unsuitable for decking and flooring. You would need to proceed with caution with these items.

[62] The Red List. *The IUCN Red List of Endangered Species*. URL: http://www.iucnredlist.org/details/38166/0 Date accessed: 3 June 2018. It is not listed under CITES at the time of writing.

[63] A good source of local names given against the botanical names and the trades can be found at http://www.daff.qld.gov.au/26_5509.htm . Date accessed, 9 July 2012.

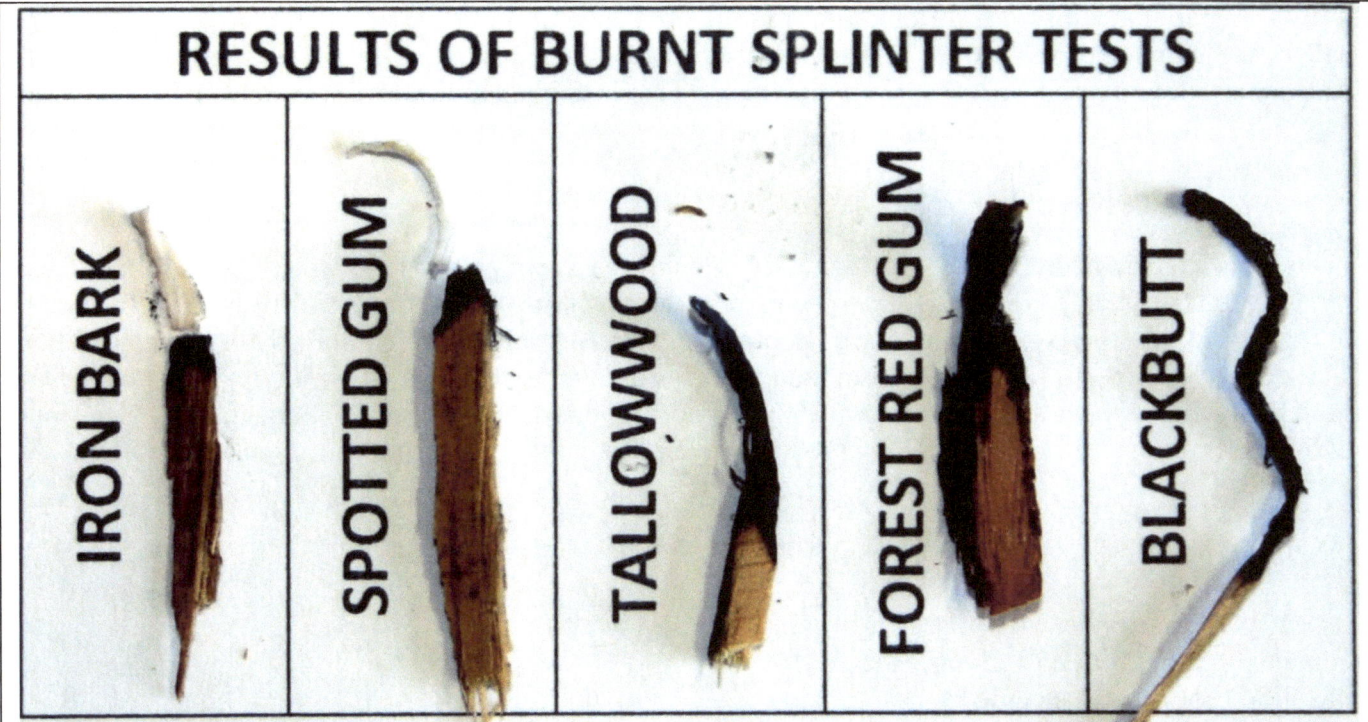

Fig. 56. Examples of burnt splinter test.

Species:	Results of Burning splinter tests
Spotted Gum	Burns to a complete white ash
Tallowwood	Charcoal tip with grey or white ash
Forest Red Gum	Burns slowly to charcoal with no ash
Blackbutt	Burns to charcoal with no ash
Red Iron Bark (narrow leaf)	Generally Burns to Charcoal

Table 6. Identifying timber with the burning splinter test.
Source DPI Forest Service Timber Species Notes 14, 16, 37, 9, 57.

The word "generally" in front of the iron bark results indicates that the test is not foolproof. The sample of Iron bark burnt almost like spotted gum but it remains a useful test. To be absolutely certain what species you are dealing with you can engage the services of what was the old Forestry Department in Queensland which will identify samples.[64] Those who are more adventurous could carefully prepare a sample of the end grain and compare it to the pictures of end grains of Australian hardwoods on the North Carolina State University Inwood database.[65]

A/NZS 4491 Timber-Glossary of terms in timber related Standards
One deviations from this standard has very important consequences for designers. This is discussed in *1.4 Definitions* and in the discussion of included heart in *1.4.4* below.

1.4 Definitions
There are 22 definitions that relate to timber grading which are basically, but not completely drawn from AS/NZS4491 Timber - Glossary of terms in timber related Standards. What is very frustrating is having

---

[64] To avail the services of their botanists, send a matchbox sized sample to Dept of Agriculture, Fisheries and Forestry, 50 Evans Rd Salisbury 4107. The fee in 2012 was $193.55 inc GST. The phone number was 07 3274 1849.
[65] The North Carolina State University Inwood database was found at http://insidewood.lib.ncsu.edu. Date accessed, 10 July 2012.

the two timber standards with different definitions for the same thing. The difference in definition of heart in the two standards has very serious consequences. Understanding this difference is one of the most important lessons to be learnt from this book. This is explained in detail my notes on clause 1.4.4 below

1.4.3 Exceptionally low density material

A new definition is added to the 2007 standard which is "Exceptionally low density material" i.e. less than 75% of the average density for a species or a species with an average density below 300 kg/m^3 (about double the weight of balsa wood). In practice with Australian timbers this is not a consideration as low density timber is rare and even radiata pine has an average density of 545 kg/m3.[66] No timbers are actually listed with a density anywhere approaching this in Table A1 of the standard, Seasoned Hardwood Species. It is difficult to comprehend anyone actually considering using such material.[67]

1.4.4 Heart

If specifying the timber you expect to get was not enough of a challenge, the relaxation of the included heart allowance in the 2007 edition of AS2082 made things even more complicated. If you are concerned about appearance and performance of weather exposed timber this section is of vital concern. You will need to get your mind around something very complex. The 2007 change means that designers requiring high performance, appearance grade hardwood must carefully consider their allowances for heart-in material.

Figure 57. 150x150 heart-in timber supplied to manufacture bollards.

The earlier standards only allowed boxed heart in sections greater than 175x175 mm in structural hardwood.[68] The heart had to be encased centrally. This meant that a conforming 150x150 mm had to be supplied free of heart. The 2007 new standard, now allows heart in many of the commonly available species from Queensland.[69] The restriction is that the heart must not exceed one ninth of the cross sectional area for Structural Grade 2, i.e. for an F17 150x150 mm the heart, which can now be at the edge, cannot exceed 28 mm in diameter.

But, what is heart? AS-NZS4491 Timber, Glossary of terms in timber related standards defines it as "timber adjacent to or including the pith that is within 50 mm of the centre of the pith", i.e. a section 100 mm boxed about the heart. That is simple and is in keeping with our experience and rules out any heart

---

[66] Hopewell. *Construction 2...*, 51.
[67] While it is theoretically possible to define groups lower than S8, timber below 390 kg per M^3 is generally too soft for normal use. Kloot. *Strength...*, 3.
[68] AS2082-2000, Clause 2.1.2 (e) (ii), Clause 2.2.2 (e) (ii), Clause 2.3.2 (e) (ii), Clause 2.4.2 (e) (ii).
[69] Clause 2.2.2. (e) (B) (ii)

in a 150x150 mm. That means heart has now shrunk to almost a quarter of that under the usual definition. The problem is that AS2082-2007 redefined the meaning of "heart". It is now "the growth centre (pith) of the tree and/or timber adjacent to the growth centre of the tree that exhibits fungal attack, brittle heart and compression failure".[70] Despite being a miller for 25 years and a qualified grader I do not know how to interpret that clause nor do I know anybody who does.

The Note to the clause mentioned says "The allowance in item (ii) only relates to the primary structural properties of the timber. **For applications where appearance or other serviceability issues are important it may be appropriate to restrict inclusion of heart, pith and heart shakes**" (emphasis mine). That means the responsibility lies with us as the supplier if we know the application and performance expectations as well as you the designer, to ensure material fit for use is received. In practical terms there is much more opportunity for unsuitable material to be supplied and it will be more difficult to shift responsibility to a producer who will simply say he was not made aware of the higher expectations. Despite warning designers since 2007, I have only seen a specification restricting heart happen once.

Figure 58. Brittle heart in 150x150.

Another difficulty is the wording "exhibiting ... brittle heart".[71] It should be assumed that all heart in material *possesses* brittle heart. Generally it does not *exhibit* it at the time of grading, it just becomes evident after installation. My publications recommend designers not specify structural 150x150 mm apart from a few feature pieces. When specified, they need to be noted that they are to be free of heart and the specification must be enforced. Even then I have too often seen substitution with heart in material.

For structural timbers, 150x100 mm should be be used in preference. Bollards should be either 125x125 mm which can be supplied free of heart (but will need to be specified that way) or 175x175 mm heart centre (better still use my Pioneer Post) with a metal cap. This is better use of a very limited resource and will also virtually eliminate the possibility of the substitution and inappropriate use of heart-in material and the awarding of the contract to "conforming" but unsuitable timber. The visual effect will be very similar. Where the client is adamant that 150x150 mm is required for a large quantity of bollards, heart centre material could be accepted but with the addition of a cap. Grading and species are still extremely important but lower performance must be accepted. The way to detail 150x150 mm heart in bollards is explained in more detail in the guide, *The Seven Deadly Sins of Timber Design*.

1.5 Timber Species and Stress Grades

Tables A1 to A4 list the relevant properties for most timber species that will be encountered in Australia. This is not an exhaustive list and there will be species encountered that are not in this list. Providing that a strength group can be established in accordance with AS2878 Timber - Classification into strength groups, the standard can be applied to them as well. Alternative, timber of the quality that will be supplied can be in-grade tested in accordance with AS4063 Characterization of structural timber.

---

[70] Clause 1.4.4.
[71] Clause 1.4.4.

Special provision is made in the standard for a special grade called A17 made from a mixture of exclusively Victorian grown timber sold under the marketing name "Victorian ash", a mixture of mountain and alpine ash. This is explained in more detail in Chapter 3.

1.6 Structural Grades of Hardwood

The F ratings are based on matching the strength group of a species with one of the four structural grades in AS2082. The structural grades are meant to represent a percentage of the strength of timber when free of any natural feature. Those percentages are found again in Table Seven. Note how low the percentage is for some grades. What makes the difference in percentage is the amount of natural feature that each of the grades allow.

I would have trouble with my conscience if I supplied some of these grades[72] because I know what they represent.[73] Yet we see some professional designers, who just see a number with an F in front of it asking for grades that are far lower than 38% of the strength of solid timber[74]. Visually and structurally they are appalling.

Structural Grade:	% of clear wood strength
No. 1	75%
No. 2	60%
No. 3	48%
No. 4	38%

Table 7. Structural grades as a percentage of solid wood.

There are, however, Structural Appearance Grades (Clause 2.5) but they only partly address the issue of appearance and are only suited for internal use and with non discerning clients.[75] The suitability of AS2082 to specify handrails is examined in Chapter 4.

1.7 Sizes and Tolerances

Over the years we have found that many specifiers have trouble with timber sizes and it is not surprising as they can be very complicated. The following will make the matter somewhat clearer. I have used 150x50 mm spotted gum as the example.

Rough Sawn Green Off Saw

This can best be understood as an approximate size only. AS2082 allows hardwood, on the day of milling, to be cut with a tolerance of + or – 3 mm. This means that 150x50 mm can be supplied anywhere between 147x47 mm to 153x53 mm. Remember, these measurements are on the day of milling only. Shrinkage then takes place as the timber seasons. This can vary between 6% (spotted gum) to 13% (turpentine). Specifications that just say F14 etc. are of no assistance as they do not refer to shrinkage, or other critical performance criteria including durability, stability or effectively deal with appearance. Our Deckwood and Joistwood specification took into consideration both performance and appearance factors.

---

[72] But for one momentary lapse – refer Appendix 1.
[73] What engineer designing a structure on the coast, exposed to the weather, would specify steel, not only without any corrosion protection but already so badly rusted that it only has 38% of its strength left. Yet this is done with timber all the time and somehow it is timber's fault when it fails.
[74] Refer to my comments on F14 and F17 KD specification.
[75] I am thinking of heartache I encountered with a job where the couple were solicitors and the wife had an extreme emotional response to a small amount of tight gum vein when the standard allows unlimited amounts in F27 KD blackbutt.

Sized Green Off Saw

This is the same product as above except that it has passed through a planer and all been reduced to the minimum size allowed under the AS2082 i.e. 3 mm undersize. A tolerance of + or - 0.5 mm applies. The timber is frequently sized for height only but at the clients request can be machined on a face and edge. This is not dressed timber as a side and an edge are often left undressed, The timber is all 147x47 mm and shrinkage still occurs. Even if sized on all four sides it should not be considered a dressed product in the sense of being meeting aesthetic requirements. Sizing is only done to structural products such as bearers and joists.

Dressed Green Off Saw

The timber can be dressed on all four sides (DAR) and would not have pencil round edges unless specified (DPR). It is normally finished 5 mm under the nominal size. If you specify 150x50 dressed, the timber will normally be supplied as 145x45. If you nominate 145x45 the producer will understand this to be the finished size. It is not generally possible to have fractional sizes cut i.e. cut slightly oversize so you can finish 150x50. What has always frightened me is that an overzealous compliance officer will one day come around and measure the timber and realize that it is 2 mm outside of AS2082 and condemn the lot. Dressed timber should be of a higher grade (F22 in spotted gum) than structural so it is not a real problem.

The standard advises that you do your calculations on say, 145x45 mm[76] but invariably it is always specified as 150x50 mm dressed.

Dressed Seasoned

This is where the biggest problems come in as, very often, the dressed, green off saw sizes are nominated and it is simply not possible to produce them. As well, some designers use the letters KD (the abbreviation for kiln dried) almost as a throwaway line e.g. 200x200 KD. Consider the following:

- It is impossible to economically dry anything beyond 50 mm thick
- unless you are prepared to wait years for the sun to season the timber, it is not very environmentally friendly to kiln dry. Kiln drying involves creating a lot of green house gases. If you are consistent in your attitudes to climate change, you must anguish before you write the letters KD.

The way to calculate the finished size is as follows; deduct the sawing tolerance – 3 mm, then deduct the shrinkage for the species, (spotted gum is 6%) and then a further 2 mm for dressing e.g. 150 mm – 3 mm tolerance = 147 mm, less 6% shrinkage = 138 mm then allow 2 mm for dressing = 136 mm. The machining tolerance of 0.5 mm applies depending on product. Table Eight should be helpful

---

[76] Clause 1.7.1 (b) Note 1.

Nominal Size	Sawing Tolerance	Green Sized	Green DAR*	Dressed Seasoned
25	+/- 3 mm	22	20	19
38	+/- 3 mm	35	33	31
50	+/- 3 mm	47	45	42
75	+/- 3 mm	72	70	66
100	+/- 3 mm	97	95	90
125	+/- 3 mm	122	120	113
150	+/- 3 mm	147	145	136
175	+/- 3 mm	172	170	160
200	+/- 3 mm	197	195	183

Table 8. Standard sizes of Australian hardwoods with 6% shrinkage.

Note on Unit Shrinkage

Something needs to be said about the forgotten measurement, unit shrinkage. This is a major consideration with flooring but it has some relevance to AS 2082 where the amount of undersize outside of the tolerances allowed is 0 mm.

The normal definition of shrinkage relates to the percent change in cross section (not length) for a piece of timber from green off saw to 12% moisture. Kiln drying introduces something few are aware of – Unit Shrinkage. This is the percentage change in cross section for each percentage change in moisture content and you can expect the timber to fluctuate by 3% during the year. This is the same for new or 100 year old recycled timber. Unit shrinkage is a critical figure when dealing with flooring but of no consequence with decking. An air conditioned environment may lower the moisture content by a further 3% below Equilibrium Moisture Content (EMC) which is why acclimatization is critical prior to laying. Unit shrinkage for spotted gum is 0.38%. So the calculation for a nominal 150 mm wide board (or an exposed joist etc) KD and dressed to 136 mm is as follows - 136 mm wide x 3% moisture content change over the year x 0.38% = 1.55 mm fluctuation in dimension over the year. This is why we strongly advise against wide T&G floor boards as, even though they may look good, customer expectation can be that the boards do not gap. Conversely, if the wood is over-dry it can swell as the climatic conditions change and the floor can grow, physically pushing the walls out. When doing a confirmation grading with a zero tolerance for undersize you are going to encounter undersize material and allowance will have to be made regardless of what the standard says.

The effect of the undersize allowance can be significant. For a time we were purchasing and processing sawn cypress. Invariably the orders would come through for F7 70X35 mm studs and plates (ex 75x38 mm). In this size cypress F7 was a hard grade to produce. But one day it dawned on me that the cypress standard allowed me to be 4 mm undersize. I asked our consulting engineer, "What happens if we actually produce without any undersize material?" The answer was that F5 cypress framing, if sold full size 75x38, could be substituted for F7. We called it Super 7 cypress.

1.7.3 Special Straightness requirements

The straightness requirements are said to relate to serviceability, not structural issues. Certain items can be ordered relatively straight such as studs and lintels but items such as bearers are supplied to very generous limits of bow and spring. An important consideration is always, "how straight does a piece of timber have to be to be serviceable in a given application. Some members can be straightened; some cannot easily be straightened without causing difficulties.

1.8 Moisture Content

The moisture content of KD framing, unlike that of flooring is not especially critical. A wide range is allowed, aiming for most of the parcel being 15% or less but with 10% of the parcel being as high as 18%. Our Australian hardwoods generally start shrinking at about 25% and shrink at a constant rate until they reach 12%, which is where measurements of shrinkage are taken. At 18% only half the shrinkage has occurred.

The most accurate way to test for moisture is by the oven dried method. This can involve cutting up the needed product to obtain the samples needed to make the test. Not a good idea. The most practical thereafter is a resistance type meter which uses prongs that are driven into the timber. To make this work you need to know the species (as the metre is calibrated to Douglas fir) and the temperature and make the necessary adjustments. From my experience, electronic capacitance meters can be less accurate and you still need to know the species and make adjustments. Without this information the readings can be misleading to the point of being all but pointless.

Moisture content tests are to be conducted in accordance with AS/NZS 1080.1. An example of why reference to this standard is necessary is with spotted gum kiln dried framing with a moisture reading taken at 30 degrees C. The target moisture might be 12%. The meter reading is 16% which is outside of the acceptable range. Alarm bells immediately ring but a trained operator deducts 2% for the increase in the reading due to the temperature and then takes a further 2 degrees off for species adjustment. The answer is 12%, i.e. the timber is at the target range. It is easy to understand complications arising when people purchase inexpensive[77] meters and use them without understanding.

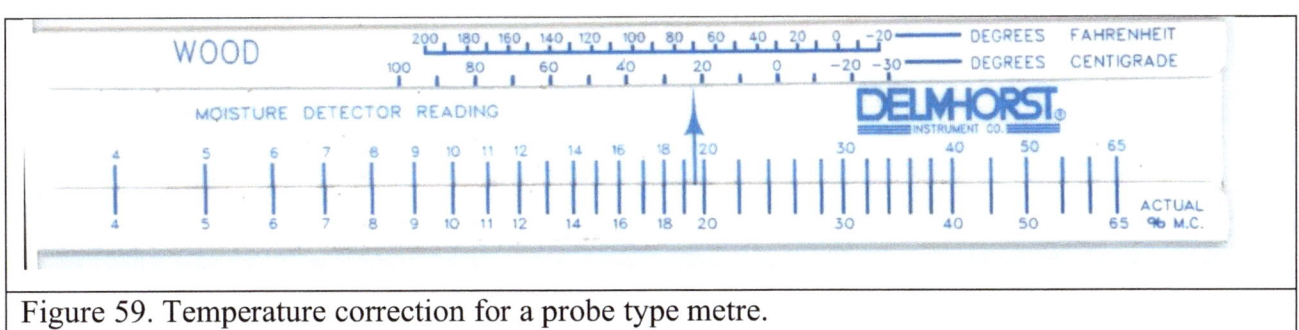

Figure 59. Temperature correction for a probe type metre.

The standard points out that the different state Acts may have a different requirement, which indeed they did/do. There is not one size fits all answer to moisture content. Our premises in Gatton in the Lockyer valley is very close to the Toowoomba Range. Local conditions are such that below the Toowoomba

---

[77] I found them available on eBay for as little as $25.00

Range the moisture content range is 12 to 15% and above the Toowoomba Range 10-12 % is needed. That made drying very awkward. A piece of 200 deep spotted gum will have shrunk about 6mm by the time it reaches 18%. It will shrink another 6mm by the time it reaches 12% but, if it was to be sent out west where the equilibrium moisture content is about 8% then you could expect a further shrinkage of 2.5 mm[78]. Where shrinkage is an issue, on site acclimatisation should be specified.

It is necessary to do your homework as some maps are too general. When I first entered the industry, moisture contents were based on shire boundaries. The map of Queensland in Figure 58 shows how this moisture can vary dramatically in a relatively short distance. This is without considering the micro environment. A timber movement calculator is available on the free website www.timberanswers.com. This tool allows you to enter species, dimensions, and location and will call up EMC and potential movement (shrinkage or swelling).

---

[78] Based on a unit shrinkage of 0.4% Tangential. DPI Forestry Timber Species Note ?

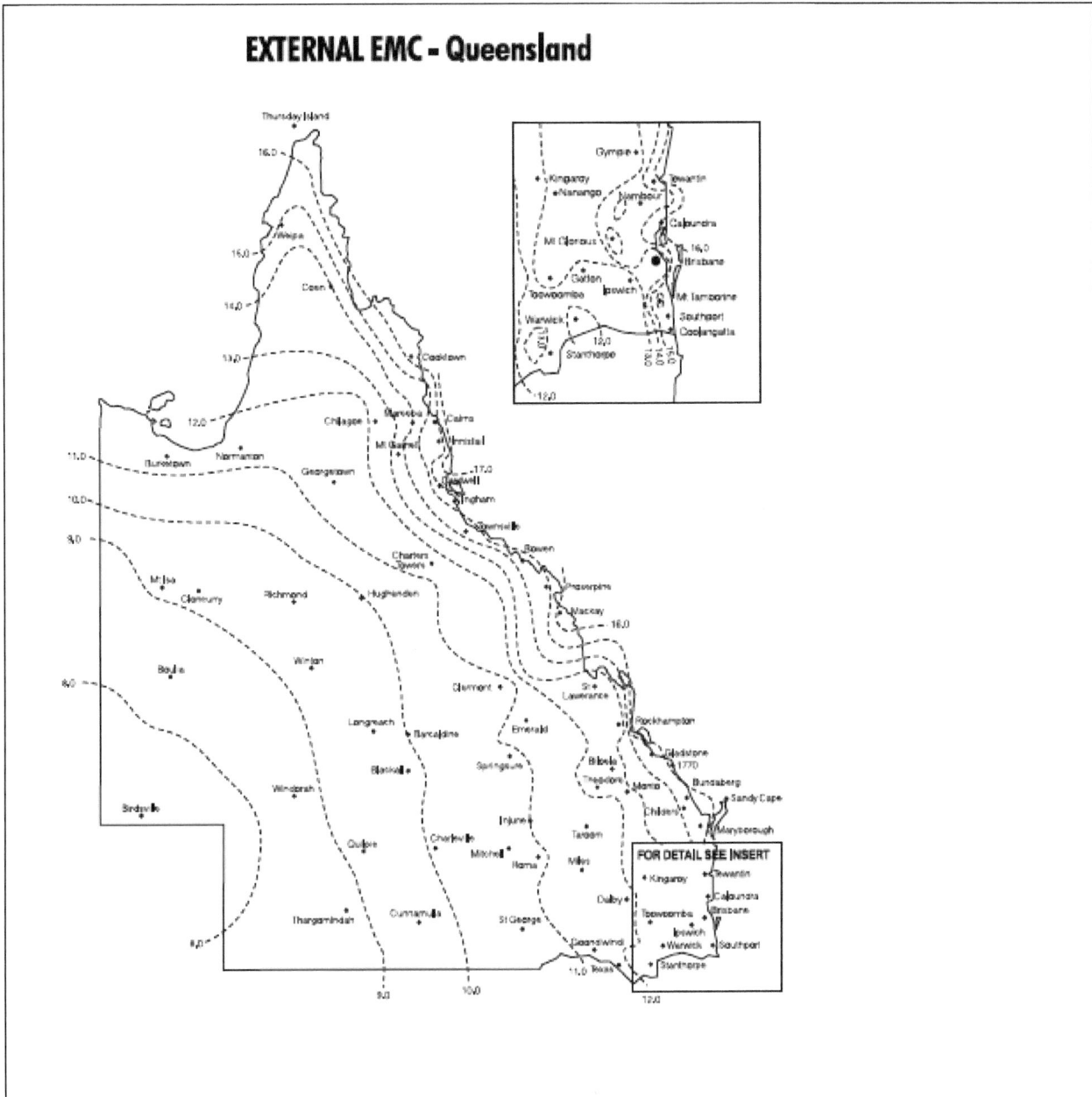

Figure 60. Equilibrium moisture content zones in Queensland (external environments; note that indoor EMC = 5/6 x external EMC).

Chapter 3. Section 3 A17.

The timber of two southern species, alpine ash (*E. delegatensis*) and mountain ash (*E. regnans*) are so similar in appearance that they are packaged together under the marketing name, Victorian ash. They share many similar properties such as fire hazard, joint group, hardness toughness, joint group and are both S4 timbers. The complication is that as these are high shrinkage timbers (alpine ash 8.5%, mountain ash 13.3% tangential), so much of the product needs to be sold kiln dried. After drying, mountain ash increases in strength to SD3 while alpine ash is only SD4. This causes complications in grading as what would be F17 in KD mountain ash would be only F14 in alpine ash.

The answer to this problem for the mixture of two species, when sourced from Victorian native forests,[79] was to treat them differently and establish a grade called A17. Gunns, a former manufacturer of this grade said of it, "Rigorous external quality audits and greater spanning ability makes GoodWood SUPA 17™ superior to traditional F17".[80] The grading rules for A17 are set out in section 3 of AS2082. F17 in KD alpine ash, the weaker of the two species is produced from Structural Grade 2 timber. The F17 and A17 grades are compared in Table Nine along with F14. In effect, the A17 timber is achieved by grading to the lower Structural Grade of S3 instead of S2. The only real difference between the A17 and Strength Group 3 grading rules is that no lyctus susceptible sapwood is permitted in A17.

Grade	knot	3 mm Borer holes in 100x100	Slope of grain	Loose gum veins	Gum pockets on one face[81]	End split aggregate
F17	1/4	20	1 in 10	1/6 of length	1/3	100mm
A17	1/3	unlimited	1 in 8	1/4	1/2	150mm
F14	1/3	unlimited	1 in 8	1/4	1/2	150mm

Table 9, Simplified comparison of F17 and F14 alpine ash to A17.

Strength groups are based on Australian wide averages for a given species. The Victorian producers were, in effect, able to establish that their timber was stronger than that from Tasmania and so, with in grade testing, justified a change in the grading rules. It is wise marketing and responsible management of the resource. This is what we did with our Deckwood. You could not describe this as a quality piece of timber, compared to what is available, but it is functional, providing you do not attempt to use it for something that needs superior properties such as verandah joists. I have seen it used as decking in Queensland! More of this is said in the following Chapter.

---

[79] Both species are found in Tasmania and alpine ash is found in South East NSW. Timber from these states is excluded from this grade.
[80] Gunns Timber Products *Gunns Structural Timber, Sustainable Australian Hardwood & Softwood*. P.4. There is no publication data on the booklet. Gunns no longer produce this product.
[81] Measured radially

Matters Arising

F17 and F11 KD Hardwood Specification

Figure 61. F17 KD hardwood.

Figure 62. F17 brand with suppliers name removed,

There was a grade of timber known loosely in the trade as *hippie grade*. The older readers will remember these people, unusual clothes, unusual hairstyle, sometimes unusual hygiene and definitely unusual cigarettes. They would purchase timber that had been rejected by people who themselves would only buy second class. Hopefully none of my readers would ever specify *hippie grade* but it is happening with increasing frequency hidden under AS2082 as F17 and F11 kiln dried hardwood! The site where these kiln dried F17 illustrated in Figures 59 and 60 above were taken, had a new structure built where the decking was specified as our Deckwood but the joists were initially specified as F11 kiln dried. This is two grades lower than that shown. (Further the joists were to be either 125 or 100x50 mm, sizes that will split due to fastener damage refer to Figure 61).

Three things affect timber grades:
- the inherent strength of the species used,
- the amount of natural feature in the timber and
- whether the timber is green off saw or kiln dried.

Each hardwood timber species is given a Strength Group (S) rating e.g. broad leaf red ironbark is S1, spotted gum is S2, forest red gum is S3 and teak, marketed as a premium timber is as low as S6. Timber quality varies dramatically too and I have described the four grades recognizes under AS2082, with Structural Grade 1 being the highest quality and Structural Grade 4 being the lowest. Industry standard grading is Structural Grade 2. To understand what these grades mean refer back to Figure 33 which shows the theoretical cross section of F11 to F22 green of saw spotted gum. With the lower grades, there is no connection between the amount of defect allowed and what designers expect to receive. Table seven showed the strength of the timber by structural grade compared to that of timber without any natural feature.

The effect of kiln drying is to effectively increase the strength of most South East Queensland timbers appropriate for external use by two Strength Groups. So when the strength group, structural grade and moisture content are known, by looking at Tables B1 and B2 in the appendix of AS2082, one for unseasoned timber and the other for seasoned timber we can determine an F grade. So, for unseasoned spotted gum we can have eight possible grades as found in Table Ten.

	Structural No. 1	Structural No. 2	Structural No. 3	Structural No. 4
Unseasoned:	F22	F17	F14	F11
KD	F34	F27	F22	F17
Table 10. Different grades achievable with spotted gum.				

Structural Grade 2, a reasonable structural grade (but definitely not an appearance grade) produces F17 in green off saw spotted gum and the same grade in kiln dried is F27! What should be then said about F17 kiln dried in spotted gum or even blackbutt which, by working backwards is the lowest grade that is conceived of? It is simply the reject of an F27 run (remember F17 kiln dried spotted gum is only 38% strength of solid timber). Further what do we say about F11 kiln dried in the same species? It is two grades below anything ever conceived of and would be about 25% the strength of solid timber. Clearly your clients deserve better.

Figure 63. Underside of 100x50 joist. Notice the split along the length of the joist!

What of those 50 mm F11 joists mentioned? We advised the architect that the joists were not according to our technical guides and that not only would they split down its length as the screws had to be in a straight line, if 100 mm thick was used, they could be expected to split from face to face as well. My competitor came along and said "Problem"? "What problem"? and got the order. I would expect that in a few years time the screws will start to come out and be a trip hazard. It is tragic.

Specification of low quality timber leads to premature failure and precludes any successful tender by a supplier with appropriate grades. At the end of the day weather exposed timber structures should not be designed for strength but for durability and when you do this you find F grades mean very little

F17 Seasoned Decking.

OSA did not recommend the use of F17 Seasoned/Kiln Dried hardwood Decking for boardwalks. For example, unseasoned spotted gum, an ideal species for boardwalk construction, is classified as a Strength Group 2 and when supplied in Structural Grade 2, F17 is achieved. If the timber is broad leaf red ironbark, the same structural grade results in F22 timber. However the timber increases in strength when dried and the same timber becomes F27 and F32. If you specify F17 seasoned the Structural Grade for spotted gum is Structural Grade 4, an extremely low grade of timber, and the lowest recognised grade. It is off the scale for ironbark. The cross section also decreases by about 6% as the timber dries

It is not just semantics as there is a company supplying F17 seasoned hardwood and in species that would normally be considered inappropriate e.g. New England blackbutt. There is a very real opportunity for inappropriate timber to be used. The lowest grade that should be considered for KD decking is F27.

Specifying Timber Handrail

| Figure 64, OSA's Queenslander P4 handrail system with OSA grabrail. | Figure 65. OSA C4 Bikeway rail with extra grabrail and kerb' |

How do you specify timber for handrail according to AS2082? Quite frankly, we ignored it and just produced a product suitable for application. What is the correct way to specify it when you do not have access to your own sawmill? In Table Eleven, two species (spotted gum and broad leaf red Ironbark) in two of the best grades (F22 and F17 exposed) are compared.

Defect	F22 SG	F22 RI	F17 EXP SG	F17 EXP RI
Want and wane	10%	20%	No	No
Gum pockets	300 mm	300 mm	No	No
Loose gum veins	1/10th length	1/6th length	No	No
Tight gum veins	Unlimited	Unlimited	Unlimited	Unlimited
Sound knot	21 mm	38 mm	38 mm	50 mm
Termite galleries	Surface	Surface	No	No
Table 11. Comparison of different grades suitability for handrail				

Neither standard is completely suitable for specifying handrail. The exposed grade with unlimited tight gum veins and up to a 50 mm knot is too generous. Timber Queensland confirmed my conclusion. A suitable specification for dressed timber handrail would be something like this:

Royal Species (including spotted gum), Structural Grade 1, Treated to H3, the order to the timber supplier is to state that the timber is required for select handrail and to over-order by 10%. (This allows for 5% of the timber supplied being out of grade[82] and a further 5% is allowed for defects that are below the surface and will be exposed when the timber is dressed). While this might seem extravagant it really only means that a few of the longer lengths need to be ordered. The cost of setting up a planer a second time if you are a piece short is usually more than having spares.

---

[82] AS 2082 2007 1.10.3

Chapter 4. Alternate Standards.

Occasionally, different Australian Standards and Industry Standards are mentioned. The following section assesses their suitability and looks in detail at the standard for recycled timber due to the increasing frequency its specification.

AS3818.6 Visually graded Decking for wharves and bridges

I never supplied decking to this specification as I believed it is inappropriate. This decking is intended for heavy commercial use with tyred traffic, not foot traffic. Timber produced to this standard is normally used with a bitumen running surface so the extent of gum vein is immaterial. To succeed as pedestrian decking a much tighter specification is needed.

AS3818.7 Visually Graded Large Section Timbers

When comparing AS2082 and AS3818.7 *Timber - Heavy structural products - Visually graded Large cross-section sawn hardwood engineering timbers* my assessment is that they both have merit and in some regards AS3818.7 is to be preferred. The alternate standard only has two grades which is either for structural or exposed use which is exactly how the timber will be used. This avoids the possible specification of one of eight grades under AS2082 and some of these are unacceptable for use. This standard only applies when the cross sectional area is at least to 0.016 m^2 which is larger than 200x75 mm and includes 150x150 mm. Given the smaller size of sawlogs now, a designer should be trying very hard to keep their sizes to a maximum of 200x75 and ideally smaller. Table 12 compares a 3.6 m length of 150x150 mm spotted gum under the two grades of AS3818.7 with three grades in AS2082, F17 a standard grade, and F22 and also with the appearance grade requirements.

Defect	AS2082-2007			AS3818.7-2010	
Grades	SG 2 F17	SG1 F22	SG1 + App F22 App	Standard (F17)	Appearance (F22)
Heart centre	Yes	No	No	No	No
Sound knot	37 mm	21 mm	21 mm	37mm	25 mm
Unsound knot/hole	37 mm	21 mm	No	25mm	25 mm
Want/wane	1/5 x section	1/10 x section	1/10 x section	1/5 x section	1/10 x section
Borer holes <3mm	20 in 100x100	12 in 100x100	12 in 100x100	unlimited	unlimited
Termite galleries	1/5 xsection	1/10 x section	No	Up to 25mm deep	Up to 25 deep
Loose Gum veins	1/6 length	1/10 length		300mm per 2 metre	300mm per 2 metre
Rot	150x100x3	150x100x3	No	No mention	No mention
Bow/Spring	13 mm	13 mm	13 mm	25 mm	25 mm
End split	100 mm	100 mm	100 mm	180 mm	108 mm

Table 12. Simplified comparison of 150x150 spotted gum at 3.6m using AS2082 and AS3818.7

The problem will be, not with AS3818.7 as such but getting a mill to supply to a different standard when you have enough troubles getting timber graded to AS2082! Their graders are seldom trained in the less common standard (if trained at all or even have a copy of AS2082 let alone AS3818.7), A course is not offered by Queensland based trainers though Timber Training Creswick Ltd do offer it.[83] Rob Rule, the Manager of Timber Training estimates that the ratio for training is 20 to 1 for AS2082 and AS3818.7. Unless you are only dealing with specialist suppliers, and you won't be if you are getting three prices, it would be wise to avoid it and, for framing timber, not decking, keep to AS2082. You will need to remember where to be careful about specifying permitted heart Decking is a completely different matter.

AS2796.1 Timber – Hardwood – Sawn and milled products

AS2796 Part 1 is the product specification for items such as flooring, lining and joinery products. Because it covers light decking it sometimes is called up for decking in boardwalks and other purposes. How appropriate is this standard? As one of the members on the committee that wrote AS2082 described it this way to me. "Would you purchase an expensive piece of furniture and then put it out in the rain?" The answer is obvious. It is a standard for joinery and appearance grade and normally kiln dried products.

But what of the crossover between this standard where AS2082 used (incorrectly) for heavy decking whereas AS2796 includes light decking? Domestic decking has traditionally been used under a roof which is a much easier application. This product performs poorly in the weather which is why we developed LifePlus, a domestic decking intended to be used in full sun.

---

[83] Their course is mainly for railway timber but adjust as necessary to the client's needs. While most of their trainees are in NSW and WA these courses are offered Australia wide.

Specifications for Recycled Timber

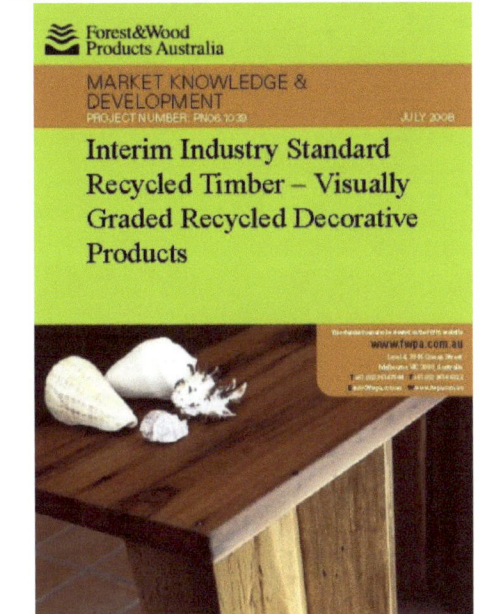

Figure 66. Interim Industry Standard Project PN06 1039 Decorative recycled

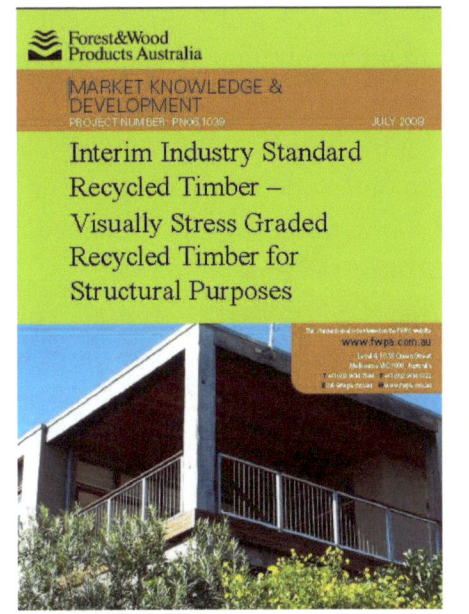

Figure 67. Interim Industry Standard Project PN06 1039 Structural Recycled

Figure 68. Recycled timber used as character pieces. Image courtesy of Guymer Bailey Architects

Increasingly, we find designers are specifying recycled timber. My recollection of the introduction of recycled timber is that architects were initially using timber salvaged from old bridges etc. to introduce "character pieces" into their creations. Invariably these pieces cost up to three times that of new timber which was expensive enough. But over time its popularity increased to the point that the word "recycled" was sometimes little more than a throwaway line, just like the letters KD with little thought to the implications of this specification. Specifying recycled timber may be done:

- to get green points for a public building or
- for the more nebulous but still important "warm and fuzzy" feeling that comes through doing something that is perceived as being responsible, or
- it could just be simple conformity.

While it is very easy to write the word "recycled" there are some serious structural and aesthetic implications that need to be thought through. A good example was the phone call I received from a very frustrated builder about a recycled job that had gone wrong in a southern state without the consumer protection of a *Timber Utilisation and Marketing Act*. He explained how he installed 200 sq m of walling which was specified as and supplied in recycled spotted gum shiplap cladding. It had shrunk so badly that, in places, the top of the board was completely clear of the shiplap. The young builder urged me to stress upon my newsletter readers how important moisture content is even with recycled timber. It is all Timber Design 101, fairly basic knowledge that somehow seems to be often overlooked.

Figure 69. Unseasoned recycled cladding shrunk out of lap

There are Interim Industry standards for recycled timber which designers will, fairly logically, refer to instead of calling up AS2082. These are *PN06.1039 Structural* and *PN06:1039 Decorative*.[84] Based on problems observed in the field, the interim standard for **structural** recycled timber while having many strengths, also has serious limitations, to the extent that it should have a major revision. In fact, we do not believe this Interim Industry Standard should be used at all for some structural products. Some tweaking is also needed for the decorative standard. This is not surprising as they are, after all, interim standards.

Figure 70. This material not suitable for decking, it is dangerous!

For applications such as handrail and decking the normal requirements of AS2082 Structural Grade 1 (face only for the decking) should apply. Specifying the ubiquitous F14/F17 is too low a grade to provide safety for the public as Figure 70 illustrates. A select piece of seasoned broad leaf red ironbark will produce F43 and for spotted gum it is F34. Remember confirmation grading is not to check if the timber is fit for purpose but whether it meets the specification! The use and specification of recycled timber as decking is expanded upon in the Guide, *Deck and Boardwalk Design Essentials* but basically the grading requirements should not be relaxed.

---

[84] Viewed at http://www.woodsolutions.com.au/fwpa/article_downloads/Recycled_Products_Structuralproducts.pdf and http://www.fwpa.com.au/sites/default/files/PNA006-607_Research_Report_Recycled_Products.pdf Date accessed: 31 August 2013.

Figure 71 shows 100x100 mm recycled boxed heart used as structural bridge handrail and was failing. At the time the timber was supplied, AS2082-2000 did not allow included heart in timber under 150x150 mm, in even the lowest quality conceivable.[85] Timber with included heart was never considered suitable for structural weather exposed rails even with new timber. It would have been classed as dunnage, i.e. disposable packing timber. Timber like this has no F rating and it is impossible to design with it. A standard that can be called upon as an authority that permits this should not be used in

Figure 71. Bridge handrail made from 100x100 with heart in the centre. Heart shake is visible.

your specification. A note needs to be made on the plans that structural members are to be supplied to AS2082. The 2007 revision of AS2082 does allow included heart and this is expanded upon in my comments on 1.4.1 But even a very generous reading of AS2082 would not allow this timber. Generally speaking, heart-in timber should be restricted to 175x175 mm and better still 200x200 mm as the heart is more enclosed.

What follows is comment on the Interim Industry Standards for recycled timber and where designers, need to be cautious and, if necessary, specify outside of that standard.

Scope 1.1 of PN06.1039 <u>Structural</u> Standard

Figure 72. Worn out timber used to construct new access bridge which quickly failed.

Appendix F of PN06.1039 (structural) shows applications that have limited human contact such as rafters and posts which we see as a good application for recycled timber. The designers' reasons for choosing recycled in these applications remains primarily aesthetic. There will be little effect from weathering. The scope however does not restrict their application in areas where structural and safety issues must over ride aesthetics. The consequence of using worn out timber in structural applications is shown in Figure 72 where low grade recycled timber was used as a bridge structure. It failed soon after construction and I was asked where expert

---

[85] Clauses 2.1.2 (e), Clauses 2.2.2 (e), Clauses 2.3.2 (e), Clauses 2.4.2 (e),

opinion could be found for a legal case.

Preservative Treatment 2.7 of PN06.1039 <u>Structural</u> Standard

Most recycled timber is taken from either:
- 50 year-old (plus) bridge timber where the sapwood has already decayed a long time ago and therefore there is no advantage in treating.
- Old powerpoles where the sapwood has already been treated and nothing more can be done. They will be CCA treated and, unless all sapwood is removed, you are may well be running foul of the intent if not the letter APVMA restrictions when using it.
- Internal timbers with sapwood that is not lyctus susceptible. The outside of this timber has "case hardened" and will not treat using normal treatment cycles. Few will be aware of this.

Designers can be left with a false sense of security that they are specifying something useful if they include reference to treatment. This could see internal timbers used externally because someone has inappropriately stamped them H5.

Scope of 1.1 (a) PN06.1039 <u>Decorative</u> Standard

Flooring is covered under the decorative standard, not the structural standard. Surely flooring is primarily structural unless the wording is changed to "flooring laid over a structural substrate"

Seasoning in section 3 2.3 PN06.1039 <u>Decorative</u> Standard

For a standard covering flooring, the wording covering moisture content is not as clear as is needed. It says in 3.3.2 *This Standard does not impose any specific moisture content requirements on these members* thinking of large cross section members. Because of safety concerns with bare feet, let alone the issue of shrinkage, we believe flooring should be supplied strictly in accordance with the Product Specification of AS2796 Timber Hardwood Sawn and Milled Products. Fortunately the Industry Standard does refer back in 3.1 (a) to AS2796 but requires the supplier to remember back a few clauses (a concern in itself) and cross reference standards. We have always found this a little dangerous. You will be amazed at the number of calls we get from manufacturers asking "what does the standard say".

Interestingly, if our southern friend who had severe shrinkage in his cladding (Figure 69) had followed the fine print in the Industry Standard he would have initially seen (as mentioned) that the Industry Standard makes reference to *AS 2796 Timber Hardwood Sawn and Milled Products*. The scope of that standard specifically mentions dressed "cladding". He could have seen that AS1684 The *Timber Framing Code* (which is a companion document to the Building Code) calls up AS 2796. The framing code mentions specific products e.g. flooring, and though cladding is not specifically mentioned neither is it excluded. So through a convoluted path it is very likely the protection against the use of unseasoned cladding eventually comes under an Act of Parliament.

It is a bit complicated for a poor old sawmiller like me, I just know it is unconscionable (at least mine) to supply unseasoned timber for chamfer boards when everything you know says it should be seasoned. Note that weatherboards are an unseasoned product.

2.3.1 Moisture Content Small End-Section Timber, <u>Structural</u> Standard

In this section, seasoned timber is specified for small end-sections, *"at least 90 percent of the pieces being graded shall have a moisture content of not more than 15 percent and no piece shall have a moisture content greater than 18 percent."* Small end section is defined as less than 0.012 m^2 (e.g. 200x50 mm). These moisture contents are far too high for anything other than decking laid with a small gap. Spotted gum shrinks 0.38% of its cross section for every percentage change of moisture content. 150 mm wide shrinking from 18% to 10% has 4.5 mm movement and almost 3 mm for 15% down to 10%. A note to this clause in the Industry Standard says *"The requirements of State timber marketing Acts (QLD and NSW) may be more stringent than those in this Standard"*. Our southern builder had no Act to call up and I am afraid, for our Queensland and now NSW readers, your government in its wisdom has repealed your Acts. Be very careful.

Shrinkage in Large End Section Timber

The standard only mentions shrinkage in small end section timber, but what about large end sections? A designer rang me about a problem he had with some recycled 200x200 mm Durability 1 in ground bollards. He was supplied with turpentine which quickly shrunk a full 10% potentially leaving finger traps between the caps and the post (this could easily develop into a litigation nightmare) as well as being unsightly. There is an expectation that timber cut from old girders/piles is seasoned when instead it acts just like green off saw timber. The cross section of round timber is simply too large to season. If say 200 mm decking is cut from turpentine piles it will shrink at least 20 mm and probably more and take the deck well outside of that permitted under the disability code. This is not theoretical, it has happened!

Shrinkage has to be addressed very clearly when you are dealing with recycled timber.

Chapter 5. How effective is grading to AS2082?

My poor old father had been a builder like his father before him and then became a sawmiller. He really had trouble with F rated timber. Where he had been supplying say, an ungraded 150x75 bearer for a certain span in our non cyclonic area, overnight that changed to a 200x75 F14. "What are they thinking." he would say "The logs are getting smaller and the timber sizes are getting bigger. The houses he and his father built with the smaller sizes were then and still are as sound then as they day they were built. But of course what he was supplying was F22 or F27 if graded to AS2082. It would have been in fact higher again as the real structural properties of our South East Queensland timber are higher than the theoretical values usually attributed to them. There probably was not much difference between his ungraded 150x75 mm and the theoretical properties of an F14 200x75 mm.

The standard "works" in the sense that members do not fail because everything is over-graded. This is particularly true for South East Queensland timbers as they are sold at F grades well under their actual properties. In 2002 the Queensland Government sponsored a review of grading of sawn timbers produced in a range of species from a number of sawmills. These mills were subject to the 1998 South East Queensland Forests Agreement. The results were published by the Department of Primary Industries as *Structural Hardwood Grading - Maximising the Potential of Structural Hardwoods Through Improved Knowledge of Characteristic Properties – Summary Report*.

It was believed that 85% of production was sold at F14 and only 15% was sold as F17. The study showed that 95% of the production could have been graded to F17 when using the Standard. When the timber was physically tested in a laboratory it was found that 95% of production exceeded the properties of F22.[86] The report concluded that "AS2082 poorly sorts structural hardwood into grades with increasing structural properties".[87]

The report's assessment of the standard itself included:
- There was a 1 in 3 chance that visually grading could actually identify the fault that would cause failure
- Timber rejected as non structural would had "residual structural properties that are suitable for use in F14+ grades"[88]
- The grading rules are too complex to reliably apply considering the education and skill level of many sawmill employees.
- The standard is a mixture of strength and serviceability issues which confused graders

As far as defects were concerned it was found:
- "Borer holes, gum pockets, heart, gum veins and overgrowth of injury are generally being over-graded.
- Sloping grain and wavy grain are generally being under-graded.
- Defects affecting structural properties are slightly more noticeable in seasoned hardwood.
- Knots, heart and overgrowth of injury have the greatest effect on bending strength
- Sloping Grain and wavy grain have the greatest effect on bending stiffness
- Sloping Grain and Wavy Grain limits can be made more efficient.

---

[86] Department..., *Structural*, 15.
[87] Department..., *Structural*, 23.
[88] Department..., *Structural*, 23.

- A Characteristic Area Ratio (CAR%) assessment method can be used for heart, overgrowth, insect damage, decay, want and wane and combinations of these defects in SEQ hardwood.
- A Knot Area Ratio (KAR %) assessment method can be used for SEQ hardwood and should come under a CAR% assessment system". [89]

The outcome of the study was a recommendation that the South East Queensland mills should transition from F grades to proposed Q grades. Only Q14 and Q22 were envisioned for Unseasoned and Q17 and Q27 for seasoned. These had slightly better properties than their F substitutes. This was achieved by restricting the species used. It was thought that this would give a better return to the millers and see the limited resource used to its maximum.

As logical as this proposed outcome was, the industry never adopted it. The logistical issues were considerable but not insurmountable. It was thought that the industry had become focused on appearance products such as flooring.[90] The real obstacle was probably the fact that it mainly Government funded so ultimately the industry did not have the degree of ownership is should have. This was basically the approach we took with Deckwood and Joistwood.

So, at this stage designers generally have access to material with structural properties well in excess of that which they are specifying.

.

---

[89] Department..., *Structural*, 23-24.
[90] Stringer, Geoff. *Pers. Com.* 18 September 2013

Chapter 6. Case Histories.

Sunshine Plaza Deck

One of the decks at Sunshine Plaza in Maroochydore has decking that is a reproduction of my Deckwood in cross section but not in quality. By going with a copy, the client did not avail themselves of our expertise in laying out a deck and basic information such as width to thickness ratios that do not cup. This was probably the lowest quality decking material that I had ever seen. It did make it easy to photograph in one spot all the defects that a grader can be expected to encounter.

I do not know what grade the decking was supposed to be so I have compared the different F grades and Deckwood.

Figure 73. Deck at Sunshine Plaza.

Sound Knot. At least it was when it was cut and that is how you have to imagine it when you grade it, not as you see it now, It measures about 60mmm across a face of 145 mm when laid, i.e. 40% of the face. The allowance for knots in AS2082 in unseasoned timber for the different stress grades is

Grade	Ironbark	Spotted Gum
F22	36mm (1/4)	21mm (1/7)
F17	48mm (1/3)	36mm (1/4)
F14	54mm (3/8)	48mm (1/3)
Deckwood	18mm (1/8)	18mm (1/8)

The knot illustrated meets no structural grade, even the lowest conceivable, and will continue to degrade. Notice the "starburst" that developed after sawing.

Figure 74. Sound Knot.

Unsound Knot. Treat as knots as in the table above. There is a pocket of resin associated with a knot. Over time the resin will degrade and wash out and leave a trap for heels

Figure 75. Unsound knot.

Combination Defect. When grading these defects the width of the knot is added to the width of the shake. This combination defect is over 50% of the piece

Figure 76. Combination Defect.

End splits near screws. This splitting is a design, not a quality issue. Our Deckwood Design Guide describes best practice on page 3. There simply is not enough room on a single joist to join as you would do lineal domestic decking that is nailed. We recommend a double joist with 150 mm between the joists and laying the deck with a 6 mm gap between the ends of the boards to prevent moisture ingress. See

Figure 77. End split due to design fault.

Tight Gum Vein. This is different to an open gum vein as there is interconnecting tissue attached to both sides of the vein. When exposed to the weather these veins always separate. The permitted amount of tight gum vein is tabled below.

Grade	Ironbark	Spotted Gum
F22	Unlimited	1/4 of length
F17	Unlimited	Unlimited
F14	Unlimited	Unlimited
Deckwood	Slight	Slight

Figure 78. Tight gum vein.

Shelling Out. Shelling out occurs when there is delamination between the growth rings. These have sharp splinters that have to be made safe as soon as they are seen. This example of delamination, which is going across the boards was evident at the time of production and should have been docked out

Figure 79. Shelling out – radially.

Shelling Out. A different form of shelling out was also visible Occasionally some boards shell out along the length and can raise sharp edges. These are not evident at the time of production and laying but occur soon after, You simply have to look for them, make them safe and replace the board. This can be in the range of 1 to 3% of the total. The practice with Deckwood is to supply replacement timber but not install them. To my knowledge no one else replaces material that has shelled out as the material was in grade when supplied.

Figure 80. Shelling out – longitudinally.

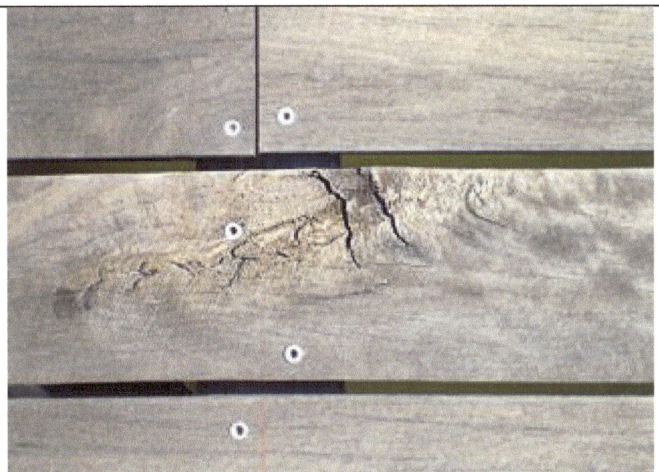

Cross shake (fracture) in conjunction with a knot. Fractures are not permitted at all under AS2082 .This defect covers over half of the board. Again this meets no F rating.

Figure 81. Cross shake.

End Split. The end split allowed under AS2082 is 100 mm. This split is at least 300 mm but probably was not like that when produced. The way this piece has split is reminiscent of the behaviour of high shrinkage timbers that are restrained with screws. By not nominating the acceptable group of species and ensuring that you receive what you ask for, you can receive timber that shrinks up to 13%.

Looking at the growth rings pattern on the face this is probably associated with heart. As well screws should have been in 35 mm from the edge so the stresses from shrinkage are not as great.

Deckwood only uses species that have 6% shrinkage.

Figure 82. End split associated with heart.

End Split Associated with Heart. This is a hard one for the uninitiated. Notice how the timber down the split is a lighter colour and there is a small knot in it. This is characteristic of heart. AS2082 forbids any heart at all but in reality the decking can carry a touch on the back. But definitely there should be none on the front.

Figure 83. End split associated with heart.

Cupping. The decking was 145x35 mm. In my first email newsletter (July 2009) I described how to minimise deck cupping and it is all down to width to thickness ratio and 145x35 mm does not work. If it must be 145 mm wide then it must be 45 mm thick. If it is 35 mm thick then it is no more than 120 mm wide. We used to make 145x35 mm a long time ago until we had two claims against it. One we had to pay on, the second was where the client knowingly used it against our recommendations. We refused to pay on that claim. That was enough. We will not make a 145x35 mm Deckwood now.

The permissible amount of cupping is 1 mm for every 50 mm for all grades so this is just in grade to AS2082 but unfit for purpose as it holds moisture, is then slippery and degrades more quickly.

Figure 84. Cupping.

All grades of timber allow rot measuring 3 mm deep and an area equal to 150x100 mm. This piece was out of grade for any structural purpose.

Primary rot should not be allowed on the face of decking as it will retain moisture and hasten the decay.

Figure 85. Rot.

Bremmer River Boardwalk, Ipswich

Figure 86. Bremmer River Boardwalk

When the extension to the riverwalk was being built in Ipswich along the Bremmer River, someone said to me, "Ted, they are using brush box for the decking." "They would not be that silly" I thought, but the asset owner needed to be advised if it was correct so I went to check. Fortunately they were not, though I have seen this substitution occur. The timber was in fact red ironbark, a royal species, often very similar in colour to brush box but it was, from my testing, as totally unfit for service as if it had actually been brush box as the top face was dressed. Comments made relate to the timber decking only.

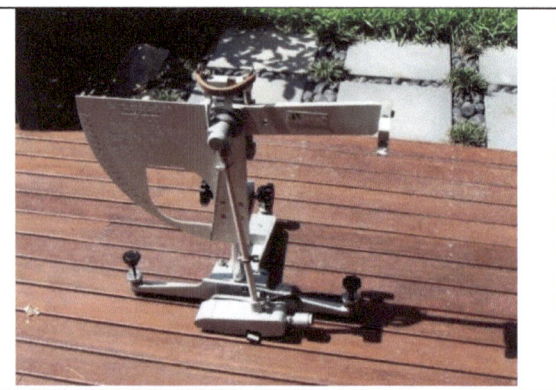

Fig 87. Slip Resistance testing on oiled dressed decking.

When photographing this deck I met someone from the construction company doing an inspection. He told me the timber was F27 which red ironbark in Structural Grade 1 will achieve. I advised the timber was not to grade and he simply walked off. We will grade this deck as claiming to be Structural Grade 1.

When grading timber you grade a batch of timber. If you are grading timber intended for a set of roof trusses that is reasonable. The standard allows for 5% of the batch to be out of grade by one grade and this is all accommodated in the design software. This approach is also fine when you are grading joists and bearers in a boardwalk but it is not acceptable for grading the decking. **Every piece must be suitable for its purpose as it is individual boards that can cause injury and litigation.**

Surface finish

Slip resistance of boardwalk decking is discussed in my *Deck and Boardwalk Design Essentials Guide*. Not only does the decking have to be structurally sound, it also has to meet the requirements of the disability code and it is the responsibility of any grader to point out that regardless, of what is written in AS2082, the timber is unfit for purpose. My testing showed that dressed face decking produces a surface where people are highly likely to slip. But acquiring this knowledge is not something that requires expensive testing in a laboratory; all that will do is give a value to its inadequate performance. Any

Figure 88. Dressed Finish.

experienced miller knows this as they would have had trouble with the inner boards of packs of dressed decking slipping out as they delivered to steep sites in the days before webbing straps. This is where the miller should be talking to the specifier and giving firm advice. This dressed face would be bad enough but the deck is on a slope with leaf litter, compounding the problem.

My own practice was to refuse to supply dressed face decking unless it was under a roof. The potential for litigation is just too high. Unfortunately the profile is a copy of my Deckwood. People copying most of the aspects of my profile without understanding what we did led to some very poor timber structures being built.

Untreated sapwood

Figure 89. Untreated sapwood on face.

The heartwood of ironbark is Durability Class 1 In Ground which makes it suitable for decking. The sapwood is Durability Class 4 for both In Ground and Above Ground applications. The sapwood of ironbark is basically as durable as the sapwood of pine. As the sapwood is not lyctus susceptible there is no restriction to the amount of sapwood even in Structural Grade 1 so this decking meets AS2082. If it was lyctus susceptible it would be restricted to $1/10^{th}$ of the cross section and $1/3^{rd}$ of the width of the edge on which it occurs.

As far as fitness for purpose is concerned, this sapwood is going to decay and will do so fairly quickly. This will leave the surface of those pieces where the sapwood has decayed below the surface of the adjoining boards. At 6 mm difference it represents a trip hazard under the disability code and the boards are unfit for purpose. This is why timber preservation is important even though it may have little effect structurally.

The decking was 120x35 mm. In Structural Grade 1, the largest knot should be more than 1/7th of the face or 17 mm. There were many boards that had knots (see Figure 10 also from this deck) far in excess of 17 mm. Structural Grade 4 would only have allowed the knot to be 45 mm. There were many knots far larger than this meaning the timber did not meet any structural grade at all. If grading to AS2082, only 5% of boards are allowed to be out of grade and then by only one grade. Nothing should exceed Structural Grade 2 with a knot not exceeding ¼ of the width or 30 mm. This knot virtually covers the whole face and a structural failure of this board is likely.

Figure 90. Large knots.

What is the consequence of a failure? In Queensland a father was holding his newborn baby when he stepped on a deck board that failed. He lost grip of his child who fell 3.6 m on her head onto concrete. These things are foreseeable. Imagine also if someone rides a horse on this. I have seen it happen often enough.

Termite Galleries

Figure 91. Termite activity.

We can see in Figure 91 that the decking screw which is in the centre of some termite damage has just continued to drive deep into the timber. Water will enter the galleries and the damage will continue to get worse. The depth of the termite attack should have been able to have been seen on the edge and it is graded as want and wane which for Structural Grade 1 is 1/10th of the cross section.

Gum Pocket

It is sometimes difficult to identify the defect you are trying to grade. Figure 92 is an example. Is it a gum pocket? There is gum in it. Is it an unsound knot encased in resin where the knot has fallen out? Irrespective of what it is you would grade/measure this as a knot. It is too large for F27 but probably makes F17. Despite being able to give it a grade it is unfit for purpose as this represents a trip hazard with high heels. Further, moisture will sit in this hole and the defect will deteriorate even further.

Figure 92. Gum pocket.

What is unfair about this job is that you would have expected the usual three quotes were obtained. Those mills that quoted on supplying to grade did not get the order because they were too expensive. The purchaser does not know and may not even care that his lowest price has come at the expense of conformity to grade. In the middle of a deep recession in the timber industry, failure to secure these large orders put the viability of responsible suppliers at risk.

Conclusion.

Timber is a natural product, you will never find a piece that is perfect but that can be part of the beauty of timber. I have a life outside of timber and in that life I am a lay preacher. I have said often spoken about the wisdom of Jesus being a carpenter. For 30 years, before he started on imperfect people, his life revolved around taking imperfect material and making something useful out of it.

After reading this guide to grading hardwood it is hoped that a specifier or user of hardwood can identify the various natural features that might be encountered. But if that is all that a reader has learnt then I have failed. I have tried to help my readers think critically about a piece of timber instead of blindly following a set of rules. I have succeeded when instead of finding reasons to reject every piece of imperfect timber you can say, "If I use it in such and such a manner, it will perform the task for which it is intended".

I hope also that you can think critically about the standard. It has been very much like the curate's egg, good in parts. It has allowed certainty in products such as roof trusses but over the same period has seen the widespread rejection of timber in its traditional use in weather exposed applications. By understanding the limitations of AS2082, a specifier can add to his specification to return the certainty that has been achieved in the past.

Appendix 1. A Personal Experience with Grading

This personal account gives some idea of the unacceptable visual appearance of the lower structural grades. Once when faced with quote request for F11 unseasoned hardwood I decided not to argue but to put my conscience aside and price accordingly and supply F11 as I wanted to prove a point. This represented Structural Grade 4 in blackbutt, the species supplied. After pricing the enquiry at a lower price to reflect F11 I received the order. I then instructed our mill manager to supply F11. He was unwilling to do as it went against his nature to supply such poor quality when his normal production was F22. The order went off and, as expected, the client was angry, complaining about the unusable quality I supplied. I reminded them that the grade specified and priced was F11 but that they should return any pieces to the wholesaler I dealt with for re-grading. On checking, all the pieces rejected as not meeting an acceptable standard were at least F14. None of the pieces were F11.

I told the builder that I would not credit the timber because it was supplied in excess of the grade ordered but I was prepared to sell him replacement timber at the F17 grade, which he accepted. The builder was advised in future not to be so silly as to design with and order low grade timber but to specify and pay for the grades he expected. I would not have liked to have been on the end of the tongue lashing the designer received.

Appendix 2. A Personal Experience with Straightness

When we were milling we also operated a timber yard and hardware store. Customers and some builders would invariably pick up each piece and run their eye down the length and put aside many pieces as being unfit for use. I was guilty of the same thing until I was shown how deceptive it was to site along a piece. After that I would not allow this to happen, or at least allow it to be used to select pieces. Clients would say, "How could you expect me to use that" and I would say "You can't tell how crooked a piece is by looking down it. How much do you think it is out of straight by?" That would answer say "Half an inch (12 mm)". I would then put a straightline on it and measure the bow or spring. It was always about half what they thought. The client would then accept the piece, albeit reluctantly. Eyeing along a piece for straightness amplifies the extent of the bow or spring.

Source of Images

Fig. 23.	Tight Gum Vein	G Hopewell
Fig. 46.	Lyctus damage	Trevor Smith, South Coast Home Check
Fig. 47	Lyctus Larvae	Doug Howick
Fig. 52	Spike in decayed F17	Not disclosed by request
Fig. 54	Boardwalk image	Glen Challenor, Saunders Havill Group
Fig. 55	Garo Garo	Timber Queensland
Fig. 58	Brittle heart	Chris Blackledge
Fig. 61	F17	Chris Blackledge
Fig. 62	F17 brand	Chris Blackledge
Fig. 68	Recycled timber	Guymer Bailey Architects

Abbreviations

EMC	Equilibrium moisture content
GOS	Green off saw
KAR	Knot area ratio
KD	Kiln dried
MCS	Maximum crushing strength or compression strength
MGP	Machine graded pine
MOE	Modulus of elasticity or 'stiffness'
MOR	Modulus of rupture or bending strength,
OSA	Outdoor Structures Australia
RI	Red ironbark
SG	Spotted Gum

References

Anonymous. *Dictionary of Timber Terms* (Timber Secretarial Group: Sydney U.D.).

Anonymous. *DPI Queensland Forest Services Timber Species Note 9 – Blackbutt,* (No publication data available)..

Anonymous. *DPI Queensland Forest Services Timber Species Note 14 – Spotted Gum*, (No publication data available).

Anonymous. *DPI Queensland Forest Services Timber Species Note 16 – Tallowwood.* (No publication data available).

Anonymous. *DPI Queensland Forest Services Timber Species Note 37 – Forest Red Gum.* (No publication data available).

Anonymous. *DPI Queensland Forest Services Timber Species Note 57 – Narrow Leaf Red Ironbark.* (No publication data available).

Bootle, Keith R. *Wood in Australia, Types Properties and Uses, Second Edition*. (McGraw Hill: Sydney, 1983).

Department of Primary Industries. *Structural Hardwood Grading - Maximising the Potential of Structural Hardwoods Through Improved Knowledge of Characteristic Properties – Summary Report.* (Department of Primary Industries: Brisbane, 2003).

Gunns Timber Products *Gunns Structural Timber, Sustainable Australian Hardwood & Softwood*. No publication date.

Hopewell, G (ed.). *Construction Timbers in Queensland: properties and specifications for satisfactory performance of construction timbers in Queensland - Class 1 and Class 10 buildings, Book 1*. (Department of Primary Industries and Fisheries: Queensland, 2010).

Hopewell, G (ed.). *Construction Timbers in Queensland: properties and specifications for satisfactory performance of construction timbers in Queensland - Class 1 and Class 10 buildings, Book 2*. (Department of Primary Industries and Fisheries: Queensland, 2010).

Hopewell, G (ed.). *Construction timbers in Queensland: properties and specifications for satisfactory performance of construction timbers in Queensland - Class 1 and Class 10 buildings, Book 2*. (Department of Primary Industries and Fisheries: Queensland, 2013).

Kloot, H. *The Strength Group and Stress Grade Systems* in CSIRO Forest Products Newsletter No 394 (Sept-Oct 1973) (CSIRO: South Melbourne 1973).

Standards Australia. *AS2082-1979 Visually stress-graded hardwood for structural purposes.* (Standards Australia: Homebush, 1997).

Standards Australia. *AS2082-2000 Visually stress-graded hardwood for structural purposes.* (Standards Australia: Homebush, 2000).

Standards Australia. *AS2082-2010 Visually stress-graded hardwood for structural purposes.* (Standards Australia: Homebush, 2010).

Standards Australia. *AS 2858-2008 Timber - Softwood - Visually graded for structural purposes.* (Standards Australia: Homebush, 2008).

Standards Australia *AS 3818.7-1010 Timber - Heavy structural products - Visually graded Large cross-section sawn hardwood engineering timbers* .(Standards Australia: Homebush, 2008).

Standards Australia. *AS-NZS4491-1997 Timber, Glossary of terms in timber related standards.* (Standards Australia: Homebush, 1997).

Internet Sites

Hayward David, Colin MacKenzie. *Interim Industry Standard Recycled Timber – Visually Graded Recycled Decorative Products.* (Forest and Wood Products Australia: Melbourne U.D.) http://www.fwpa.com.au/sites/default/files/PNA006-0607_Research_Report_Recycled_Products.pdf. Date accessed: 31 August 2013.

Hayward David, Colin MacKenzie. *Interim Industry Standard Recycled Timber – Visually Graded Recycled Structural Products.* (Forest and Wood Products Australia: Melbourne U.D.) http://www.woodsolutions.com.au/fwpa/article_downloads/Recycled_Products_Structuralproducts.pdf. Date accessed: 31 August 2013.

Forest Products Commission Western Australia. *Timber Advisory Notes* http://www.fpc.wa.gov.au/content_migration/plantations/species/species_notes.aspx. Date accessed: 5 July 2012.

MCM Hardwood. URL http://www.infolink.com.au/c/MCM-Hardwood. Date accessed: 5 August 2013.

Tait Flooring. URL http://www.taitflooring.com.au/pages/products/flooring/timber-types/royal-species.php. Date accessed: 5 August 2013.

TLB Timber http://tlbtimber.com.au/Timber%20Types%20and%20Grades.pdf Date accessed: 9 July 2012.

The Red List. The IUCN Red List of Endangered Species. URL: http://www.iucnredlist.org/details/38166/0 Date accessed: 3 June 2018.

About the Author

Ted Stubbersfield was born in the small Queensland town of Gatton in 1950. After studying to be a pastor in Brisbane and the UK he returned to the family business, Gatton Sawmilling Co. A fair question would be, "Can anything good come out of Gatton"? Well, Gatton was the home of a Governor General of Australia (William Vanneck 1938). It is also the home of the best and most innovative hardwood producer in Australia, Outdoor Structures Australia (OSA).

The family had been involved in sawmilling and building for about 140 years and a lot of knowledge has passed through the generations. In 1985 we ventured into the footbridge market (almost by accident) and then followed public landscaping. Initially we just did as we were told by consultants who knew very little about timber. In about 1988 Ted decided he would come to know the medium he was working with far better than any of his competitors and most of the professionals who used his products.

Ted realised that there were no useful standards and guides for designing and building weather exposed timber structures such as boardwalks. That led in 1997 to his first formal research project on boardwalk design, engineering supply and construction. Over the years there followed a complete set of guides. These allowed professionals to design timber structures of exceptional beauty and durability. Typically, everybody wants to re-invent the wheel and the guides were usually ignored. Invariably, the same mistakes keep being made over and over. This little book is an attempt to remedy this.

In 2012, the time came to close the manufacturing arm of OSA and to take on a less stressful lifestyle. Ted plans to put in writing much of what he has learnt so the industry does not have to relearn it. This book on grading hardwood is the fourth in a series of Timber Design Files that are intended to show designers how to avoid the pitfalls of common, but often bad practice as well as Standards that can be very inadequate and engender a false sense of security